The Companion Guide for Parents & Mentors to The Ultimate Devotional for Teen Boys

David Powell

CONTENTS

INTRODUCTION

As a parent or mentor, your influence is one of the most significant factors in a teen's faith journey. Walking alongside a young person as they explore their relationship with God, build character, and navigate life's challenges is a privilege and a profound responsibility. This *Parent/Mentor Companion Devotional* is designed to support you in that journey, offering practical tools, insights, and activities to deepen your bond with the teen you're guiding while nurturing their spiritual growth.

This companion guide aligns with *The Ultimate Devotional for Teen Boys*, providing you with an overview of each week's themes, Bible stories, and key takeaways. It also includes conversation starters, journaling prompts, and activities to encourage meaningful discussions and shared experiences. Whether you're a parent, grandparent, youth leader, or mentor, this guide is a resource to help you connect with your teen and walk with them in faith.

Flexibility and Freedom

The activities and conversation starters in this guide are designed to give you ideas—not rules to follow. You might use them as written, adapt them to suit your teen's personality and interests, or set them aside entirely in favor of something that fits your unique relationship. There is no one "right" way to guide a teen in their faith, and this resource is here to support—not constrain—you as you lead by example.

Feel free to mix and match the suggested activities and conversation topics. If an activity feels particularly meaningful or fun, lean into it. If a certain week's topic brings up sensitive issues, approach the conversation with honesty and grace, adapting to what your teen needs most in that moment. Your authentic presence and willingness to share your own experiences—both successes and struggles—are what will resonate most with your teen.

Partnering with God

This journey is as much about your growth as it is about theirs. Each week includes practical challenges, journaling prompts, and opportunities for reflection designed to help you deepen your own relationship with God. By prioritizing your faith and modeling a God-centered life, you provide a powerful example for the teen in your care.

You don't have to have all the answers to be a great mentor. God equips those He calls, and as you lean on Him for wisdom and guidance, He will use you to plant seeds of faith, hope, and love in your teen's life.

A Shared Journey

Faith is best nurtured in community, and this devotional is an invitation to journey together. As you engage with the lessons, stories, and Scriptures, take time to pray with and for your teen. Share your own reflections and invite them to do the same. Whether you're laughing over an activity, having a deep conversation, or simply being present, these moments build trust and create opportunities for growth.

This year-long journey is not about perfection—it's about progress, connection, and faithfulness. May this devotional guide you both closer to God and to each other, and may it help you equip your teen to live a life of faith that honors God in every season.

I pray that as you walk alongside your teen, you will experience the joy of seeing them grow in faith, character, and purpose. Together, may you discover the beauty of a life anchored in God's love and truth.

In Christ,

David Powell

WEEK 1

WHO IS GOD?

Introduction:

This week, your teen will be learning about the foundational question: *Who is God?* They will explore God's role as Creator, His holiness, love, and justice, and how they can have a personal relationship with Him. Your role as a mentor will be to help your teen see these truths in action, both through Scripture and in your own life.

Practical Challenge:

Teen Challenge: Get to know God better this week by reflecting on His character. Each day, take 5 minutes to think about one aspect of God (Creator, Holy, Loving, Just, or Personal). Write down one way you see this attribute of God in your daily life or in the world around you. Pray and ask God to reveal more of Himself to you in each of these areas.

Mentor Challenge: (Same as the teen challenge) Spend time this week meditating on God's nature — His role as Creator, His holiness, His love, and His justice. Encourage the teen to do the same, and look for ways God reveals these qualities in your daily life. **In addition:** In your Bible reading, start asking the question "What do I learn about God from this passage of Scripture?" and start taking notes about God's character.

Bible Story: Creation and the Fall (Genesis 1-3)

Reflection: Genesis 1-3 introduces us to God as Creator, the One who brought everything into existence with His words. The story of creation reminds us of the immense power and creativity of God, who made everything from nothing. But it also points us to the fall, where humanity's sin disrupted the perfection God had intended. Yet, even in the fall, God's love and justice remain evident. As adults, reflecting on creation helps us remember our place in God's world and the purpose He has for us. It also reminds us of the personal and powerful relationship He desires to have with each of us.

Key Themes:

- God as the Creator of all things.

- God's holiness and justice in response to sin.

- The importance of seeking a personal relationship with God.

Teen Devotional Recap:

- **Day 1:** *God as Creator* – Genesis 1:1 – Reflecting on God's power and creativity in creating the world and our purpose as part of His creation.

- **Day 2:** *God as Holy* – Isaiah 6:3 – Understanding God's holiness and purity and how it draws us into reverence for Him.

- **Day 3:** *God as Loving* – 1 John 4:8 – God's love is not just an action but part of His nature. His love for us is unconditional and sacrificial.

- **Day 4:** *God as Just* – Psalm 89:14 – Exploring how God's justice ensures fairness, defends the helpless, and sets things right.

- **Day 5:** *Knowing God Personally* – Jeremiah 29:13 – God desires a personal relationship with us. When we seek Him with all our hearts, we will find Him.

Weekly Summary:

This week focused on God's nature: His role as Creator, His holiness, love, and justice, and how we can know Him personally. These truths are essential for building a relationship with God and understanding who He is. As a mentor, you can help the teen grasp these concepts by sharing how you have experienced God in these roles throughout your life.

Journaling Questions for Mentor:

1. When was the first time you truly reflected on God as the Creator? How did this change your understanding of the world around you?

2. How do you respond to God's holiness? Have you ever felt a deep reverence or awe in His presence?

3. Can you think of a time when you felt distant from God but experienced His unconditional love? How can you share this experience with your teen?

4. How has God's justice given you comfort in times when life felt unfair or challenging?

5. How can you grow in your personal relationship with God this week, and how might this growth encourage your teen?

Real-Life Story

Eric Liddell: The Runner Who Honored God

Eric Liddell was a famous athlete who is known for his faith and love for God. He is often remembered for saying, "God made me fast. And when I run, I feel His pleasure."

In the 1924 Olympics, he refused to run in the race he had trained for because it took place on a Sunday, and he wanted to honor God by keeping that day for rest. Instead, he competed in a different race, which he wasn't expected to win — and won gold! Liddell later went on to become a missionary in China, where he continued to live out his faith by serving others. Eric's life reminds us that knowing who God is and desiring to honor Him and trust Him can strengthen us to make bold decisions that demonstrate His power to the world around us (Lidell, 2001).

Discussion or Activity with Teen:

Activity:

Take a walk in nature with the teen, pointing out the beauty of God's creation. Use this time to talk about how God's role as Creator impacts your faith.

or

"God in My Life Collage"

1. Gather materials like magazines, newspapers, colored paper, markers, and glue, or if you prefer a digital approach, use a phone or computer for an online collage.

2. Invite your teen to create collages with you representing different aspects of God's nature (Creator, Holy, Loving, Just) and how they see these qualities in their life or the world around them.

3. Encourage them to include images or words that symbolize God's creativity (like nature or art), His love (like family or friends), His justice (symbols of fairness or helping others), and His holiness (moments they feel connected to God).

Debrief: Once finished, discuss your collages together. Ask questions like, "Why did you choose each image or word?" and "How do these aspects of God influence how you see the world?"

Conversation Starter:

"When Have You Seen God's Love, Justice, or Creativity?"

Open the conversation by sharing a personal story where you felt God's love, observed His justice, or saw His creativity at work. Then, ask your teen:

- "Can you think of a time when you experienced or saw God's love, justice, or creativity in your own life?"

- "Which of God's qualities do you feel closest to, and why?"

- "Is there one quality of God's character that you'd like to understand better?"

This gives them a chance to reflect on and discuss how they connect with God's nature personally.

WEEK 2

GOD'S LOVE FOR YOU

Introduction:

This week, your teen will be learning about the profound truth of God's unconditional love. They will explore how His love is not based on performance, see examples of His love in the Bible, and reflect on how to recognize and respond to that love in their daily lives. Your role as a mentor will be to help your teen understand this love and guide them in accepting and embracing it fully.

Practical Challenge:

Teen Challenge: Every day this week, write down one way you see God's love in your life. It could be through a person, a circumstance, or something simple like nature. At the end of the week, review the list and thank God for each of these displays of His love.

Mentor Challenge: (Same as the teen challenge) Encourage your teen and share what each of you has noticed about God's love throughout the week. Explain to your teen that it can take real focus to change focus, from seeing the negativity around us, in order to see God's love.

Bible Story: The Parable of the Lost Sheep (Luke 15:1-7)

Reflection: In Luke 15, Jesus tells the story of a shepherd who leaves his 99 sheep to go after the one who was lost. This story beautifully illustrates the heart of God's love — a love that is willing to pursue, search, and bring back those who are far from Him. God's love is relentless, personal, and never-ending. As an adult, reflect on how God has pursued you with His love throughout your life. How did you come to experience this love? This story is a reminder that God cares deeply for each one of us, and no one is ever too far from His love.

Key Themes:

- God's unconditional, pursuing love.

- The joy of reconciliation and restoration.

- God's personal care for every individual.

Teen Devotional Recap:

- **Day 1:** *God's Love Is Unconditional* – Romans 5:7-9 – God's love is constant and unchanging, nothing can separate us from it.

- **Day 2:** *Examples of God's Love in the Bible (Jesus' Sacrifice)* – John 3:16 – Jesus' sacrifice is the ultimate example of God's love for us.

- **Day 3:** *Recognizing God's Love in Everyday Life* – Psalm 136:1 – God's love is evident in both big moments and small, everyday blessings.

- **Day 4:** *Accepting and Embracing God's Love* – Ephesians 3:17-19 – Understanding that we are worthy of God's love, and allowing that love to fill us with confidence and joy.

- **Day 5:** *Responding to God's Love Through Faith and Action* – 1 John 4:19 – God's love compels us to love Him and others in return, not just through feelings, but through action.

Weekly Summary:

This week focused on understanding God's love, which is unconditional and sacrificial. Your teen learned about the ultimate example of this love in Jesus' sacrifice and were encouraged to recognize God's love in everyday moments. They also reflected on how to accept this love and how to respond to it by loving God and others. As a mentor, you can help your teen grasp these truths by sharing how you've experienced and responded to God's love in your own life.

Journaling Questions for Mentor:

1. Have you ever struggled with feeling unworthy of God's love? How did you overcome that feeling, and how might your experience help your teen?

2. Reflect on a time when you've seen clear examples of God's love in your life. How has this changed your relationship with Him?

3. How have you personally experienced God's love in small, everyday moments? Can you share an example of this with your teen?

4. What might be holding you back from fully embracing God's love in your own life? How can you work on breaking down those barriers?

5. How can you model responding to God's love through action? What specific steps could you take this week to live out His love toward others?

Real-Life Story

Katie Davis Majors: A Heart for Loving Like Jesus

Katie Davis Majors, author of *Kisses from Katie*, was an ordinary teenager who followed an extraordinary calling from God. At 18 years old, she moved to Uganda and eventually adopted 13 young girls while starting a ministry to serve the people in her community. Katie's life is a powerful example of living out God's love, compassion, and grace in action. She says, "I have learned that I will not change the world, Jesus will do that. I can, however, change the world for one person. And if one person sees the love of Christ in me, it is worth every minute." Katie's story reminds us that God's love is transformational and that He can use our lives to make a difference in others' lives through simple acts of love and obedience (Davis, 2012).

Discussion or Activity with Teen:

Activity:

Choose an activity to do with your teen that is a little out of the ordinary to help show your love for them and to demonstrate your dedication to walking through this year with them. It could be catching a ball game together, going to a Christian concert, or just going to their favorite restaurant.

or

"Love Letter from God"

1. Provide your teen with a notebook, pen, or digital document to write down words or phrases they believe describe God's love for them (such as "unconditional," "ever-present," "patient," "sacrificial").

2. Ask them to reflect on Bible verses they know about God's love (John 3:16, Romans 5:8, 1 John 4:9-10, etc.) and think about how God shows love personally to them.

3. Encourage them to write a short "letter" or list of statements from God's perspective, as if He were expressing His love specifically for them. For example, "I am always with you," "You are my beloved child," or "Nothing can separate you from my love."

Debrief: Afterward, talk about what they wrote or felt during the activity. Ask them how these reminders of God's love might change the way they see themselves or others.

Conversation Starter:

"When Have You Felt God's Love in a Special Way?"

With the story of the Lost Sheep in mind, share a story from your life when you felt "pursued" by God's love. Begin by sharing a personal experience where you felt God's love clearly — through answered prayers, a friend's kindness, or during a challenging time.

Then, ask your teen:

- "Can you remember a moment when you felt God's love in a really strong way?"

- "How does knowing that God's love is unconditional change the way you think about yourself?"

- "What are some ways you think you can respond to God's love in your everyday life?"

These questions help open up a conversation about recognizing and responding to God's love personally.

WEEK 3

GOD AS A FATHER

Introduction:

This week, your teen will be learning about God as a loving, perfect Father. They will reflect on what it means to have God as their Heavenly Father, comparing His perfect fatherhood with human fathers and learning to trust His guidance, provision, and protection. Your role as a mentor will be to help your teen embrace this truth and see themselves as beloved children of God, even if their earthly experiences with fathers have been difficult.

Practical Challenge:

Teen Challenge: Talk to God daily as you would to a loving Father. Share your worries, joys, and dreams with Him. If you struggle to see God as your Father, ask Him to reveal Himself to you as a good Father this week. Remember that you are His beloved child. If your ideas of God as a Father are different than seeing him as a "Daddy", for example you can only picture Him in heaven, being distant, instead of close and even present, or stern and judgmental instead of loving, ask God to reveal to you any misconceptions you may have and even the source of those misconceptions and to replace those ideas with His truth.

Mentor Challenge: (Same as the Teen Challenge) Encourage your teen and share with each other how this practice deepens your relationship with God. If you are the teen's father, this is a time to ask God to show you anywhere where you have not measured up to God's standards as a father. As He shows you, repent to God and ask for forgiveness from your teen. This honesty and vulnerability will build a deeper trust and relationship with your teen. This can seem scary as a Father, but it can have an amazing impact on you and your teen.

Bible Story: The Parable of the Prodigal Son (Luke 15:11-32)

Reflection: In the Parable of the Prodigal Son, Jesus tells the story of a father who eagerly welcomes back his wayward son. This story illustrates God's fatherly love — one that is filled with grace, forgiveness, and joy. The father in the story doesn't hold his son's mistakes against him; instead, he runs to meet him, embraces him, and restores him to his rightful place in the family. As adults, this story may remind us of times when God has shown us such forgiveness and unconditional love. Reflect on how God's fatherly love has transformed your own life and how you can share that with your teen.

Key Themes:

- God's unconditional, fatherly love.

- The joy of reconciliation and restoration.

- God's readiness to forgive and welcome us back.

Teen Devotional Recap:

- **Day 1:** *What It Means for God to Be Our Heavenly Father* – 1 John 3:1 – God loves us as His children, and we are accepted and treasured by Him.

- **Day 2:** *Comparing God's Perfect Fatherhood with Human Fathers* – Psalm 68:5 – God's fatherhood is perfect, compassionate, and never failing, even when human fathers fall short.

- **Day 3:** *Trusting God's Fatherly Guidance* – Proverbs 3:5-6 – Trusting in God's guidance means surrendering our understanding and trusting that He sees the bigger picture.

- **Day 4:** *His Fatherly Love, Protection, and Provision* – Matthew 6:26 – God provides for our needs and values us deeply, more than anything else in creation.

- **Day 5:** *Living as a Beloved Child of God* – Romans 8:15 – As God's children, we live in freedom, calling Him "Abba," which means "Dad." We are part of His family and can confidently trust in His love.

Weekly Summary:

This week focused on understanding God as a loving Father who provides, guides, and cares for His children. Your teen learned that God's fatherhood is perfect, even when earthly fathers fall short. They reflected on God's guidance, protection, and love, and were encouraged to live confidently as beloved children of God, free from fear and doubt. As a mentor, your role is to reinforce this understanding and help your teen experience God's fatherly love in a personal way.

Journaling Questions for Mentor:

1. How has your understanding of God as your Heavenly Father changed throughout your life? Were there key moments that deepened this understanding?

2. How does your experience with your earthly father influence your view of God as a Father? If you've had challenges with this, how has God worked in your life to bring healing?

3. Reflect on a time when you had to trust God's guidance, even when it didn't make sense to you. How did His fatherly care and wisdom become clear in the end?

4. In what ways have you experienced God's provision and protection in your life? How can you share these experiences with your teen to encourage them?

5. What does it mean to you to live as a beloved child of God, and how can you model this confidence and trust for your teen?

Real-Life Story

Bilquis Sheikh: "I Dared to Call Him Father"

Bilquis Sheikh was a Pakistani Muslim who had a life-changing encounter with God. In her book *"I Dared to Call Him Father,"* she describes how she came to understand God as a personal and loving Father instead of a distant, angry deity. This realization transformed her life, giving her courage and peace to leave behind her old life and culture to follow Jesus, even at the risk of death in a country hostile to Christianity.

One of her most challenging times came when she started openly living out her Christian faith, which included attending church and speaking about her newfound beliefs. News of her conversion quickly spread, causing outrage among her family members and others in her community. She received threats from influential figures, warning her to renounce her faith or face severe consequences. Even her own family distanced themselves, fearing social disgrace and reprisals from the community.

Bilquis was told that her life could be in danger if she continued as a Christian. On one occasion, she heard rumors of a planned attack on her home. Despite the risk, she decided to stay, placing her trust in God's protection. That night, she prayed fervently, asking God for peace and strength. She experienced a deep sense of calm that replaced her fear, feeling God's presence with her. Remarkably, the potential attackers did not carry out their plans that night. Those who had planned to harm her later reported feeling an unexplainable reluctance to go through with their intentions, as if they were held back by something unseen. Bilquis attributed this change of heart to God's intervention, believing that He had shielded her from harm that night. Bilquis later shared that this experience reaffirmed her faith and deepened her reliance on God's provision and protection. Bilquis' story teaches us that seeing God as "Father" can change everything — bringing us into a close, life-giving relationship with God and empowering us to live boldly (Sheikh, 1978).

Discussion or Activity with Teen:

Activity:

Consider a bonding activity to have fun while talking about this week's topic. Bowling and miniature golf are fun activities that allow for conversation and bonding while having fun.

or

"Letters to Our Heavenly Father"

1. Provide your teen with a journal or sheet of paper to write a letter to God, addressing Him as "Father."

2. Encourage them to express gratitude for ways they feel God has protected, guided, or provided for them. If they struggle to identify these, encourage them to write down any qualities or actions they would want in an ideal father and how they hope to see God's fatherly love in their life.

3. Prompt them to ask God for anything they need, like guidance, protection, or peace, just as they would ask a loving father.

Debrief: After they write, ask if they'd like to share anything about their letter or how it felt to address God as Father. This helps reinforce their sense of God's fatherly love and opens the door for honest conversations.

Conversation Starter:

"What Does a Good Father Mean to You?"

Read the Parable of the Prodigal Son (Luke 15:11-32) with the teen. Ask them how they think the father's reaction reflects God's fatherly love. Share personal stories about times when you have experienced God's forgiveness or grace in your own life and encourage the teen to share any moments when they have felt God's fatherly love and care. Begin by sharing a story or example of a time you felt God's fatherly guidance, protection, or care.

Note: If you are the teen's father approach this very humbly so that your teen feels the liberty to be honest about things they might think are lacking in your relationship. Be prepared to ask for forgiveness and to be challenged with things you might need to improve. Our society teaches us to deal with these awkward moments with humor and even sarcasm, but I encourage you to avoid humor and allow an open and honest conversation that allows for vulnerability.

Then, ask your teen:

- "What do you think it means to have a good father?"

- "What would you like to be different in your relationship with your earthly father and how do you think that might affect your relationship with your Heavenly Father?"

- "Can you think of any times when you felt God's guidance or protection, even if it was in a small way?"

- "How does knowing God as a loving Father change the way you feel about your relationship with Him?"

These questions help open a deeper conversation about seeing God as a Father and trusting in His perfect love and guidance.

WEEK 4

THE IMPORTANCE OF PRAYER

Introduction:

This week, your teen will be learning about the importance of prayer in building a relationship with God. They'll explore how prayer can change both circumstances and hearts, as well as strengthen their trust in God. As a mentor, your role will be to encourage your teen to develop a regular prayer life, guiding them to see how essential prayer is to spiritual growth and daily peace.

Practical Challenge:

Teen Challenge: Set aside a specific time each day to pray this week. Even if it's just 5 minutes, make it a priority. Find a quiet place, turn off distractions, and talk to God about your day, your worries, and what you're thankful for.

Mentor Challenge: Set aside an additional time each day to pray this week, apart from your normal prayer routine. Even if it's just 5 minutes, make it a priority. Find a quiet place, turn off distractions, and talk to God about your day, your worries, and what you're thankful for. Encourage your teen in their challenge, and at the end of the week, discuss how setting aside time (or additional time) for prayer impacted both of you.

Bible Story: Daniel and the Lion's Den (Daniel 6:1-28)

Reflection: In Daniel 6, we read about Daniel's unwavering commitment to prayer, even when faced with the threat of death. Despite the king's decree forbidding prayer, Daniel continued to pray three times a day. His faithfulness to God resulted in miraculous protection when he was thrown into the lion's den. This story demonstrates the power of prayer and the trust we place in God through consistent communication. As adults, we often face pressures and challenges in life, yet Daniel's story reminds us that prayer is the key to staying connected to God and trusting Him in the face of trials.

Key Themes:

- The importance of consistent prayer.

- Trusting God's protection and provision through prayer.

- The power of prayer in difficult circumstances.

Teen Devotional Recap:

- **Day 1:** *Why Prayer Is Essential in Building a Relationship with God* – Revelations 3:20 – Prayer connects our hearts to God, allowing us to share our thoughts, fears, and hopes with Him.

- **Day 2:** *The Power of Prayer to Change Our Hearts and Circumstances* – James 5:16 – Prayer has the power to change both our situations and our hearts, giving us peace and strength.

- **Day 3:** *Jesus' Example of a Prayerful Life* – Luke 6:12 – Jesus often withdrew to quiet places to pray, showing us the importance of prioritizing time with God in the midst of busyness.

- **Day 4:** *How Prayer Strengthens Our Trust in God* – Psalm 55:22 – Prayer helps us cast our burdens on God and grow in trust as we see His faithfulness in response.

- **Day 5:** *Making Prayer a Daily Habit* – 1 Thessalonians 5:17 – Building a habit of prayer keeps us in constant connection with God throughout our day.

Weekly Summary:

This week focused on the importance of prayer as the foundation of our relationship with God. Your teen learned that prayer not only changes circumstances but also transforms their hearts, helping them trust in God more deeply. Jesus' life serves as an example of the priority of prayer, and the challenge this week is to cultivate a daily habit of staying connected with God through prayer. As a mentor, you can help your teen understand how prayer strengthens their faith and gives them peace, even in difficult situations.

Journaling Questions for Mentor:

1. How has prayer impacted your relationship with God throughout your life? What seasons of life have deepened your prayer life?

2. Can you think of a time when prayer changed either your circumstances or your heart? How can you share this experience with your teen to encourage them?

3. What do you find most challenging about maintaining a consistent prayer life? How have you overcome these challenges?

4. Reflect on Jesus' example of prioritizing prayer in His busy life. How can you create more intentional space for prayer in your daily routine?

5. How does prayer strengthen your trust in God, especially in difficult seasons? How can you model this trust for your teen?

Real-Life Story

George Müller: A Life of Prayer

George Müller was a Christian evangelist known for his dedication to prayer and trust in God. He took care of thousands of orphans in 19th-century England without ever asking for donations — he simply prayed for God to provide. And God always answered in amazing ways, often at the last moment! One famous story of God's miraculous provision in George Müller's life happened one morning when the orphanage had run out of food entirely. Müller gathered the children and staff together in the dining hall, and they prayed, thanking God for the food they were about to receive—even though there was none.

As they finished the prayer, there was a knock at the door. When Müller opened it, the local baker stood there, explaining that he had felt God leading him to bake extra bread for the orphanage in the early hours of the morning. He had brought plenty to feed everyone. Just as the bread was being handed out, there was another knock at the door. This time, it was the milkman. His cart had broken down right outside the orphanage, and he explained that the milk would spoil by the time he could get the cart fixed. So, he offered all the milk to the orphans for free. In that single morning, the orphans received both bread and milk—enough to satisfy everyone. This moment is one of the many times George Müller recorded instances of God's timely provision, made possible through prayer and faith. Müller's life is a powerful example of how prayer can change not only personal circumstances but also impact the lives of countless others (Müller, 1984).

Discussion or Activity with Teen:

Activity:

Do some research ahead of time (Open Doors and Voice of the Martyrs are good places to start) and lead your teen to pray for the persecuted church. Find some websites with testimonies and stories that show Christians today live with the same persecution and faith as Daniel in the Old Testament. After reading these stories and understanding the need, pray together for the persecuted church.

or

"Prayer Journal Challenge"

1. Provide your teen with a journal or notebook specifically for prayers.

2. Encourage them to write down a few specific things to pray about each day this week — for themselves, others, or even the world. Each entry can include:

   ○ A few sentences or words about what they're thankful for.

   ○ Any worries or challenges they want to lift up to God.

   ○ Something they're curious about or want to understand better in their relationship with God.

3. At the end of the week, have them look back at their entries to see how they felt God's presence and any ways He may have responded to their prayers.

Debrief: Ask if they noticed anything about their feelings, thoughts, or relationship with God through their journaling. This helps reinforce the idea of staying connected with God in all areas of life.

Conversation Starter:

"What Do You Think Prayer Changes?"

Begin by sharing a personal story of a time when prayer gave you peace, clarity, or strength in a challenging situation, or you can also start by sharing from your thoughts on Daniel 6.

Then, ask your teen:

- "What do you think happens when we pray? Do you think it's more about changing situations or changing us?"

- "How has prayer helped you before, or is there a time you're curious about trying prayer for something specific?"

- "If you had to describe your relationship with God in one word right now, what would it be? How do you think prayer could strengthen that relationship?"

These questions encourage them to think about prayer not just as a practice but as a way to grow in their faith and trust in God.

WEEK 5

HOW TO PRAY

Introduction:

This week, your teen will be learning practical ways to pray, using the ACTS model, being honest with God, praying for others, and listening for His voice. They'll also explore how to prioritize prayer in the busyness of life. Your role as a mentor is to help your teen see prayer not as a ritual, but as an essential part of their relationship with God, and guide them to make it a regular practice.

Practical Challenge:

Teen Challenge: Continue with the challenge from last week, but this week choose one time each day to spend 5-10 minutes in prayer using the ACTS model. Write down any thoughts or things you feel God speaking to you, and be sure to take a few moments in each prayer to listen for His voice.

Mentor Challenge: (Same as the Teen Challenge) Encourage your teen and discuss what you've both learned at the end of the week.

Bible Story: Hannah's Prayer (1 Samuel 1:9-20)

Reflection: Hannah's story in 1 Samuel 1 is a powerful example of heartfelt, honest prayer. Deeply grieved because of her inability to have children, she pours out her heart to God in the temple, and her vulnerability is met with God's grace. Her prayer is raw and open, expressing both sorrow and hope. God not only hears Hannah's prayer but answers it in a way that blesses her and glorifies Him. Hannah's story reminds us that prayer is not about presenting perfect words, but bringing our true selves before God, trusting Him with our deepest desires and struggles.

Key Themes:

- The power of honest and heartfelt prayer.

- God's faithfulness in answering prayer.

- Trusting God in both prayer and waiting.

Teen Devotional Recap:

- **Day 1:** *Understanding the Basics of Prayer (ACTS: Adoration, Confession, Thanksgiving, Supplication)* – Matthew 6:9-13 – Using the ACTS model helps us focus on praising God, confessing our sins, giving thanks, and asking for our needs.

- **Day 2:** *Being Honest and Open with God in Prayer* – Psalm 62:8 – God desires honest prayers, where we pour out our hearts and trust Him with our true feelings.

- **Day 3:** *Praying for Others — Intercessory Prayer* – 1 Timothy 2:1 – Intercessory prayer allows us to partner with God in bringing His will into the lives of others.

- **Day 4:** *Listening for God's Response* – John 10:27 – Prayer involves not just speaking but listening for God's voice, recognizing how He communicates with us.

- **Day 5:** *Finding Time for Prayer Amidst a Busy Life* – Psalm 5:3 – Setting aside time for prayer, even in a busy life, helps us stay connected to God throughout the day.

Weekly Summary:

This week focused on practical aspects of prayer, including the ACTS model, honesty with God, praying for others, listening for God's response, and making time for prayer. Your teen learned that prayer is not about using perfect words, but about connecting with God from the heart. As a mentor, your role is to help your teen see the beauty of daily communication with God and to model the importance of listening and praying for others.

Journaling Questions for Mentor:

1. Have you ever used a specific model for prayer, like the ACTS model? How has it helped or changed your prayer life?

2. Reflect on a time when being honest with God in prayer made a difference in how you approached a difficult situation. How can you share that experience with your teen?

3. Who are some people you regularly pray for, and how has intercessory prayer impacted your relationship with God and others?

4. How do you hear God's voice in prayer? What steps can you take to create more space for listening in your prayer life?

5. What practical changes can you make to prioritize prayer in your daily routine? How can you help your teen find time for prayer in their life as well?

Real-Life Story

Brother Lawrence: Practicing the Presence of God

Brother Lawrence, a monk in the 1600s, discovered the beauty of connecting with God through prayer in everyday life. In the monastic tradition he was a part of, there were designated times throughout the day where everyone in the monastery stopped what they were doing and went to the sanctuary to pray. However, Brother Lawrence found that he had his most profound encounters and conversations with the Lord when he began to develop the habit of "practicing the presence of God" throughout his day. He learned to pray all throughout his day, whether washing dishes or doing daily chores, and found that God would answer him and meet with him in all of those moments, not just in the sanctuary. His life is a reminder that prayer doesn't have to be limited to specific times but can be a continuous conversation with God, inviting Him into every part of our lives (Lawrence, 1982).

Discussion or Activity with Teen:

Activity:

Do a prayer walk around your teen's neighborhood and/or school together. Use the ACTS prayer model. Let the teen come up with topics they think are relevant for supplication and then add your own ideas.

or

"ACTS Prayer Guide"

1. Create an "ACTS Prayer Guide" together to help the teen become comfortable using the ACTS model (Adoration, Confession, Thanksgiving, and Supplication).

2. Divide a journal page into four sections labeled A, C, T, and S.

   ○ **Adoration**: Write down praises to God, focusing on His character (loving, just, merciful, etc.).

   ○ **Confession**: Write a sentence or two about anything they want to bring before God for forgiveness.

   ○ **Thanksgiving**: List three things they're grateful for today.

   ○ **Supplication**: Write any prayer requests — for themselves and for others.

3. Encourage them to use this structure each day this week as a framework to pray, but remind them they can pray in any order or style as well.

Debrief: At the end of the week, talk about which part of the ACTS model felt the most natural to them and which felt more challenging. Discuss any new thoughts or feelings they had about prayer.

Conversation Starter:

"What Does it Mean to Pray Honestly?"

Start by sharing about a time you prayed openly and honestly with God, mentioning how it helped you.

Then, ask your teen:

- "Have you ever felt like you needed to use the 'right' words when you pray? What would it feel like to just talk to God about whatever's on your mind?"

- "Who do you think about most when praying for others? Why do you think it's important to pray for others, even if they may never know?"

- "Have you ever sensed God speaking back to you in any way during prayer or afterward?"

These questions help them consider prayer as a real conversation with God and explore how they can connect authentically and honestly.

WEEK 6

LISTENING TO GOD

Introduction:

This week, your teen will be learning about listening to God's voice through His Word, in prayer, and through people, circumstances, and the Holy Spirit. They'll explore how to recognize and respond to God's guidance. As a mentor, your role is to help your teen develop the practice of listening for God's voice and encourage them to act on what they hear.

Practical Challenge:

Teen Challenge: Spend time in quiet prayer each day, asking God to speak to you and help you recognize His voice. Then, find one passage of Scripture to read and reflect on how God is speaking to you through it. Write down what you sense God saying and how you can apply it to your life.

Mentor Challenge: (Same as the Teen Challenge) Encourage the teen and discuss how listening to God's voice is shaping both of you. Be honest about the difficulty of learning to be still and listen as well as expecting God to speak through His Word. Also remind your teen that with our closest friends we are comfortable even in silence, and we should be able to be that way with God at times too.

Bible Story: The Calling of Samuel (1 Samuel 3:1-10)

Reflection: In 1 Samuel 3, we read about the young boy Samuel learning to recognize God's voice for the first time. Even though Samuel was living in the temple and serving under Eli, it took time and guidance for him to realize that God was speaking to him.

Samuel's willingness to listen and obey set him on the path to becoming a great prophet. This story reminds us that hearing God's voice is a process of learning and growing. As adults, we may need to be patient, both with ourselves and with the teens we mentor, as we help them learn how to listen for God's voice and follow His guidance.

Key Themes:

- Learning to recognize God's voice.

- The importance of being open and willing to listen.

- Obedience to God's direction, even when it's unfamiliar or challenging.

Teen Devotional Recap:

- **Day 1:** *God Speaks Through His Word, the Bible* – 2 Timothy 3:16 – The Bible is God's main way of speaking to us, and reading it daily helps us understand His voice and truth.

- **Day 2:** *Recognizing God's Voice in Prayer* – Romans 10:17 – Prayer is a conversation with God, and He answers us by speaking to our hearts, often bringing peace, guidance, and impressions that line up with His Word.

- **Day 3:** *How God Uses People and Circumstances to Guide Us* – Proverbs 11:14 – God often uses others or situations in our lives to direct and guide us according to His will.

- **Day 4:** *The Role of the Holy Spirit in Helping Us Understand God's Will* – John 16:13 – The Holy Spirit guides us into truth and helps us understand God's will for our lives.

- **Day 5:** *Being Open and Responsive to God's Direction* – James 1:22 – Hearing God's voice is only part of the process; we must also respond with obedience and faith.

Weekly Summary:

This week focused on learning to listen to God in various ways: through His Word, in prayer, through people and circumstances, and by the Holy Spirit. Your teen was challenged to recognize God's voice in these areas and respond with obedience. As a mentor, your role is to help your teen develop the practice of listening for God's voice and encourage them to act on what they hear. Sharing your own experiences of hearing and responding to God's voice can help the teen navigate this process.

Journaling Questions for Mentor:

1. When have you experienced hearing God's voice through Scripture? How did it impact your decisions or actions?

2. Have you ever had difficulty recognizing God's voice in prayer? What have you learned through those experiences?

3. Reflect on a time when God used a person or circumstance to guide you. How can you share this experience with your teen to help them see how God might be guiding them?

4. How does the Holy Spirit help you discern God's will in your life? In what ways can you explain this to your teen to help them understand the Holy Spirit's role?

5. Are there areas in your life where you've heard God speak, but you've hesitated to respond? How can you use this experience to encourage your teen to act in faith?

Real-Life Story:

Elisabeth Elliot: Trusting God's Voice in Hard Times

Elisabeth Elliot, a missionary and author, faced the tragedy of her husband Jim's death at the hands of the rural Ecuadorian tribe they were trying to reach for Christ. In the midst of loss, she learned to listen to God's voice for comfort, guidance, and purpose. Later, in obedience to the Lord's direction, she returned to that same tribe to share the gospel, forgiving those who had killed her husband. Her act of forgiveness and obedience led to the eventual healing and transformation of the whole tribe. Elisabeth's story teaches us that listening to God isn't always easy, but His voice leads us to healing, forgiveness, and hope (Elliot, 1989, *Shadow of the Almighty*).

Discussion or Activity with Teen:

Activity:

Do a "treasure hunt" with your teen. You both start by asking God to show you who He wants you to speak to today. Then you wait and listen. You pay attention to anything you hear or see in your mind (for example, a girl in a bright green shirt or a man with tattoos on his right elbow). After sharing with each other what you heard and or saw, then go to a pre-determined public place like a shopping mall and look for those people. If you find someone that matches, go and talk with them. Let them know that God showed them to you in prayer earlier and ask if you can pray for them. If they allow you to pray, pray for whatever requests they share, but also listen to God again to see if there is something specific He wants you to pray for for them.

or

"Listening to God Journal"

1. Encourage your teen to start a "Listening to God Journal" for the week.

   ○ Each day, they can write down any impressions, thoughts, or feelings they sense might be from God. They can note anything that stands out from their Bible reading, something they heard during prayer, advice or encouragement from others, or insights from circumstances they're experiencing.

   ○ At the end of each day, ask them to reflect on whether these thoughts align with what they know about God's character and His Word.

2. At the end of the week, meet to talk about what they noticed.

   ○ Were there any recurring themes or clear impressions?

   ○ How did it feel to intentionally listen for God each day?

Debrief: This practice helps them grow comfortable with discerning God's voice in everyday life. Discuss any insights or moments where they felt close to God or learned something new.

Conversation Starter:

"How Do We Know It's God's Voice?"

Start by sharing a time when you believed you heard God's voice and how you recognized it.

Then, ask your teen:

- "What do you think God's voice sounds like? Does it feel like a thought, a feeling, or something else?"

- "Have you ever had an experience where you felt like God was speaking to you? How did you respond?"

- "How can we know if something is truly from God or just our own thoughts?"

These questions encourage your teen to reflect on what it's like to hear from God, helping them consider how to differentiate His voice from other influences.

WEEK 7

THE BIBLE - GOD'S WORD

Introduction:

This week, your teen will be learning about the relevance of the Bible today, its structure, and how to read, study, memorize, and understand how Scripture can be applied in real, daily life. The goal is to help them see the Bible not just as a book to be read, but as a living guide meant to shape their lives and deepen their relationship with God. Your role as a mentor is to encourage your teen to engage with God's Word regularly to find guidance for everyday situations.

Practical Challenge:

Teen Challenge: Choose one verse this week to memorize and reflect on. Write it down, carry it with you, and repeat it throughout the day. Ask God to help you apply that verse in specific situations that arise.

Mentor Challenge: (Same as the Teen Challenge) Encourage the teen and at the end of the week, discuss how memorizing Scripture helped you both in real-life situations.

Bible Story: The Temptation of Jesus (Matthew 4:1-11)

Reflection: In Matthew 4, Jesus demonstrates the power of Scripture when He is tempted by the devil in the wilderness. Each time Satan tries to deceive Jesus, He responds with a verse from the Bible, showing that God's Word is a powerful tool for resisting temptation and standing firm in truth. Jesus' example teaches us that knowing Scripture isn't just an intellectual exercise — it's a weapon for spiritual warfare and a guide for life. Reflect on how Scripture has helped you in times of temptation or challenge and how it continues to shape your decisions today.

Key Themes:

- The power of Scripture in resisting temptation.

- Using God's Word as a guide for life and decision-making.

- The importance of knowing and memorizing Scripture.

Teen Devotional Recap:

- **Day 1:** *Why the Bible Is Relevant Today* – Hebrews 4:12 – God's Word is alive and active, speaking into our lives today and guiding us through all situations.

- **Day 2:** *Understanding the Bible's Structure (Old and New Testament)* – Luke 24:44 – The Bible is divided into two main sections, the Old and New Testaments, both revealing God's story of redemption and His plan for the world.

- **Day 3:** *How to Read and Study the Bible Effectively* – 2 Timothy 2:15 – Reading the Bible involves meditating on its meaning and asking God to reveal how it applies to your life.

- **Day 4:** *The Importance of Memorizing Scripture* – Psalm 119:11 – Memorizing scripture helps us carry God's truth with us, giving us strength and guidance in difficult moments.

- **Day 5:** *Applying God's Word in Daily Life* – Luke 11:28 – The Bible is meant to be lived out in our daily actions, guiding how we speak, act, and treat others.

Weekly Summary:

This week focused on why the Bible is relevant, how it's structured, and how to read, study, memorize, and apply it. Your teen learned that God's Word isn't just a book to be read but is a living guide meant to shape their lives and draw them closer to God. As a mentor, your role is to help your teen see how Scripture can be applied in everyday situations, helping them make it a central part of their spiritual growth.

Journaling Questions for Mentor:

1. How has reading and studying the Bible shaped your relationship with God over

time? What parts of Scripture have impacted you most?

2. Have you found certain sections of the Bible challenging to understand or apply? How have you worked through these challenges?

3. Reflect on a time when memorizing Scripture helped you in a difficult moment. How can you share this experience with your teen?

4. What strategies have helped you study the Bible more effectively, and how can you share these methods with your teen to help them engage more deeply with God's Word?

5. How do you ensure that God's Word isn't just something you hear, but something you live out in your daily actions?

Real-Life Story:

Dietrich Bonhoeffer: Grounded in the Word of God

Dietrich Bonhoeffer was a German pastor and theologian who stood against the Nazi regime during World War II. While in prison for his faith and opposition to Hitler's regime, he spent hours reading and meditating on the Bible. Even as he awaited his impending execution, Bonhoeffer found strength, courage, and hope through God's Word. In the darkest times, he remained grounded in biblical truth, and throughout his time in prison, he wrote letters to his friends, encouraging them in the Gospel and in God's faithfulness. The letters he wrote while in prison were published by a friend of his after Bonhoeffer's execution in a work titled *Letters and Papers from Prison*. Those letters continue to be an encouragement to believers today, long after Bonhoeffer's death. Bonhoeffer's story shows us that being deeply rooted in God's word can strengthen us to face even the gravest challenges (Metaxas, 2010).

Discussion or Activity with Teen:

Activity:

Find a Bible study app (like e-Sword) and help the teen set up the app and learn how to use the Strong's Concordance with Greek and Hebrew, dictionaries, commentaries, devotionals etc. to enhance their ability to study Scripture.

or

"Verse Application Challenge"

1. Together, select a short, meaningful Bible verse for the week — one that speaks to something relevant in your teen's life, such as kindness, trust, or patience.

    ◦ For example, *"Your word is a lamp to my feet and a light to my path."* (Psalm 119:105)

2. Challenge them to apply the verse in specific ways each day.

    ◦ Discuss possible applications. If the verse is about kindness, they might choose to show extra kindness to a friend or sibling. If it's about trust, they could pray about something they're worried about and leave it with God.

3. At the end of the week, meet to discuss how focusing on the verse impacted their choices and perspective.

Debrief: Talk about how the verse helped guide them or gave them a new perspective in certain situations. This activity reinforces that Scripture is practical and personally relevant.

Conversation Starter:

"What Does It Mean for the Bible to Be 'Living'?"

Start by sharing about Jesus' temptation in the wilderness and then how a particular Bible verse or passage has impacted you in a real-life situation.

Then, ask your teen:

- "Do you have a favorite Bible verse or story? How has it helped you or encouraged you?"

- "How do you think the Bible can be 'living' — what do you think that means?"

- "What's one part of your life right now where you think the Bible could give you guidance or encouragement?"

This conversation invites your teen to see Scripture as an active, guiding force and encourages them to share any ways the Bible has spoken to them personally.

WEEK 8

THE POWER OF WORSHIP

Introduction:

This week, your teen will be learning about the power of worship and how it's not just about singing, but about living a life that honors God. Worship connects us deeply with God and helps us focus on His greatness rather than our problems. As a mentor, your role is to help your teen understand that worship is a lifestyle — something that happens in daily life, not just at church.

Practical Challenge:

Teen Challenge: Choose one new way to worship God this week. Whether it's through singing, serving someone in need, or taking time to thank God for His blessings, find a creative way to express your worship and draw closer to Him.

Mentor Challenge: (Same as the Teen Challenge) Encourage the teen and share how this new form of worship has deepened your relationship with God. Help the teen to really recognize whatever they choose to do as worship and not just another activity. Remind them that worship doesn't come from the activity itself, but from the heart and mindset in the activity.

Bible Story: David Dances Before the Lord (2 Samuel 6:12-22)

Reflection: In 2 Samuel 6, we see King David express unrestrained worship when the Ark of the Covenant is brought back to Jerusalem. David's joy was so great that he danced before the Lord with all his might, demonstrating his love and reverence for God. This story shows that worship is not about maintaining appearances — it's about expressing our devotion and gratitude to God, even when others don't understand. David's example reminds us that true worship comes from the heart and is a powerful response to God's presence in our lives.

Key Themes:

- Worship as a joyful and wholehearted expression of love for God.

- Worshiping God with sincerity, regardless of how others view it.

- Worship as a response to God's presence and goodness.

Teen Devotional Recap:

- **Day 1:** *Worship as a Response to God's Greatness* – Psalm 95:6 – Worship is our response to who God is, honoring Him for His greatness, power, and love.

- **Day 2:** *Different Forms of Worship (Singing, Serving, Living)* – Colossians 3:17 – Worship can take many forms, including serving others and living a life that reflects gratitude to God.

- **Day 3:** *Why Worship Connects Us Deeply with God* – Psalm 22:3 – Worship shifts our focus to God's greatness and invites His presence into our lives, helping us experience His peace and joy.

- **Day 4:** *Worshiping in Spirit and Truth* – John 4:24 – True worship comes from a sincere heart and a genuine connection to God's truth, led by the Holy Spirit.

- **Day 5:** *Worship as a Lifestyle, Not Just an Event* – Romans 12:1 – Worship isn't just something we do on Sundays; it's how we live every day, offering our lives as "living sacrifices" to honor God.

Weekly Summary:

This week focused on the power of worship, not just as an act of singing, but as a response to God's greatness and a lifestyle of honoring Him in all we do. Your teen explored different forms of worship, learned about worshiping in spirit and truth, and was challenged to live out their worship daily. As a mentor, your role is to help your teen understand that worship is about more than just songs — it's about living for God with sincerity and gratitude in every part of life.

Journaling Questions for Mentor:

1. What are some different ways you've learned to worship God throughout your life? How have these practices helped you grow closer to Him?

2. Reflect on a time when worship helped shift your focus from your problems to God's greatness. How can you share this experience with your teen?

3. How do you practice "worshiping in spirit and truth" in your daily life? What does authentic worship look like for you?

4. In what ways can you make worship more of a daily practice, rather than just something you do at church? How can you encourage your teen to do the same?

5. How can you honor God more intentionally in your daily routine, seeing your life as an act of worship?

Real-Life Story:

Matt Redman: Heart of Worship

Matt Redman, a Christian worship leader and songwriter, learned the power of worship through a season where his church stripped away all musical instruments and sound systems to focus purely on worshiping God from the heart. Out of that experience, he wrote the well-known song, "The Heart of Worship." The song's lyrics remind us that worship is not about performance or appearance — it's about bringing our hearts sincerely before God. Reflecting on this season of his life, Matt once said, "In the end, worship can never be a performance, something you're pretending or putting on. It's got to be an overflow of your heart...Worship is about getting personal with God, drawing close to God" (Redman, 2001). True worship is about connecting with God and honoring Him with everything we are.

Discussion or Activity with Teen:

Activity:

Depending on where you live, take the teen to a place described in a Psalm.

For example:

Psalm 23: a forest with a stream

Psalm 46: the oceanside

Psalm 107: desert/wilderness, or shipping dock, or fields/vineyards

Psalm 121: mountains

Read the Psalm together in that location, letting the surroundings bring the Scripture to life. Meditate on God's greatness and then praise Him whether by song, word, or simple expressions of "awe".

or

"Worship Through Gratitude Collage"

1. **Gather Materials:** Have your teen gather old magazines, newspapers, or printed images, along with scissors, glue, and paper or a journal page.

2. **Create a Collage:** Encourage them to cut out images or words that represent areas of life where they see God's greatness or feel grateful — these might include family, nature, talents, or anything that inspires worship.

3. **Add Scripture:** Have them write or glue in a worship-related Bible verse (e.g., *"Let everything that has breath praise the Lord."* - Psalm 150:6) to complete their collage.

Debrief: Use this collage as a reminder that worship isn't just for Sunday or during songs; it's in recognizing and honoring God in all aspects of life.

Conversation Starter:

"What Does It Mean to Worship Beyond Church?"

Start by sharing how worship has been meaningful in your own daily life — perhaps through gratitude, service, or even in moments of reflection.

Then, ask your teen:

- "What are some things that make you feel close to God or in awe of Him?"

- "How could you turn everyday moments (like helping a friend, studying, or even relaxing) into a way to honor God?"

- "What's something in your life right now that could become a form of worship if you did it with God in mind?"

This conversation helps your teen see that worship is a continual act, where every part of life can become an opportunity to honor and connect with God.

WEEK 9

FAITH IN ACTION

Introduction:

This week, your teen will be learning about what it means to live out their faith through actions, not just words. They will explore how small acts of kindness, consistency in their beliefs, and trusting God to use their faith can have a powerful impact on others. As a mentor, your role is to encourage the teen to put their faith into practice and to help them see how their daily choices reflect their walk with God.

Practical Challenge:

Teen Challenge: Do one intentional act of kindness each day this week. It can be as simple as sharing a kind word, doing a helpful deed, or listening to someone who needs to share what's on their heart. Let your actions be a reflection of your faith and love for God.

Mentor Challenge: (Same as the Teen Challenge) Encourage your teen and discuss how these acts of kindness have impacted both of you at the end of the week. For your teen and yourself this challenge will require being intentional to look for the opportunities that show up each day. Don't be discouraged if you miss a day, just jump right back in the next day. Remind your teen that growing in our faith is a journey.

Bible Story: The Good Samaritan (Luke 10:25-37)

Reflection: The story of the Good Samaritan is a powerful example of faith in action. When a man is beaten and left for dead, it's not the religious leaders who stop to help, but a Samaritan — someone who was typically despised in that culture. The Samaritan doesn't just feel compassion; he acts on it by caring for the man and ensuring his needs are met. This story reminds us that true faith leads to action. As adults, we often find opportunities to put our faith into practice in unexpected ways. Reflect on times when you've been called to act on your faith, and consider how you can encourage your teen to do the same.

Key Themes:

- Faith that leads to compassionate action.

- Being willing to help others, even when it's inconvenient.

- Living out love for God through practical service to others.

Teen Devotional Recap:

- **Day 1:** *Living Out Your Faith Through Words and Actions* – James 2:17 – Faith isn't just something we believe; it's something we live out through our words, actions, and how we treat others.

- **Day 2:** *Examples of Faith in Action from the Bible* – Hebrews 11:1 – The Bible's "heroes of faith" inspire us to trust God even when we can't see the full picture.

- **Day 3:** *How Small Acts of Kindness Reflect Our Faith* – Galatians 6:10 – Small acts of kindness, like helping a friend or encouraging someone, reflect God's love and our faith.

- **Day 4:** *The Importance of Consistency in Living Out Your Beliefs* – Philippians 4:9 – Consistency in our faith is important because people are watching how we live, and our example can make a difference.

- **Day 5:** *Trusting God to Use Your Faith to Impact Others* – Matthew 5:16 – When we live out our faith, we become a light to others, and God uses our words and actions to draw people closer to Him.

Weekly Summary:

This week focused on living out faith in practical ways — through words, actions, kindness, and consistency. Your teen learned that faith isn't just a belief but a lifestyle. When we consistently live out our faith, God uses our daily choices to impact the world around us. As a mentor, you can help your teen see how small acts of kindness and faithfulness in their everyday life can be a powerful testimony to those around them.

Journaling Questions for Mentor:

1. How has living out your faith through actions, rather than just words, made a difference in your life? Can you share an example with your teen?

2. Reflect on a person from the Bible or from your life who inspires you to live out your faith boldly. What can you learn from their example?

3. Think of a time when a small act of kindness reflected your faith and impacted someone else. How can you encourage your teen to practice kindness as a reflection of their faith?

4. In what areas of your life do you need to be more consistent in living out your beliefs? How can you model consistency for your teen?

5. How can you trust God to use your words and actions to impact others this week? What specific steps can you take to live out your faith more intentionally?

Real-Life Story:

William Booth: Faith in Action Through Service

William Booth, the founder of The Salvation Army, devoted his life to living out his faith by serving the poor, homeless, and needy. Booth believed that faith should be active and make a tangible difference in the lives of others. He famously said, "Faith and works should travel side by side, step answering to step, like the legs of men walking. First faith, and then works; and then faith again, and then works again — until they can scarcely distinguish which is the one and which is the other" (Booth, 1890). Booth's life teaches us that our faith should be more than words; it should lead to action that reflects God's love to those around us.

Discussion or Activity with Teen:

Activity:

Set a date to volunteer together at a soup kitchen or food pantry in your area. Encourage your teen to connect with people by asking questions. The human connection will last longer than the service performed.

or

Choose a missionary biography to read together (maybe one chapter a week) and discuss how the missionary's story encourages each of you to put your faith in action.

Conversation Starter:

"What Does It Mean to Live Out Your Faith?"

Begin by sharing a story of a time when you saw faith lived out in an everyday setting — whether through kindness, integrity, or helping others.

Then, ask your teen:

- "Who's someone you know that lives out their faith in a way that stands out to you? What do they do that makes their faith visible?"

- "What are some everyday actions you could take to show kindness or integrity, even if no one else sees?"

- "How do you think living out your faith affects the people around you, even in small ways?"

This conversation can help your teen see how their actions, big or small, can reflect God's love and leave a lasting impact.

WEEK 10

TRUSTING GOD IN DIFFICULT TIMES

Introduction:

This week, your teen will be learning about trusting God during difficult times. They will explore how God is present in our struggles, how challenges can strengthen their faith, and how holding onto hope in God's promises helps them endure hard situations. Your role as a mentor is to guide your teen in understanding that even in pain or confusion, God is at work and can be trusted to bring peace and purpose.

Practical Challenge:

Teen Challenge: Identify a current struggle or challenge you are facing. Spend time each day praying about it, reading scripture related to trust, and speaking words of hope over your situation. Ask God to help you trust Him more deeply in that area.

Mentor Challenge: (Same as the Teen Challenge) Encourage your teen and at the end of the week, discuss how trusting God has impacted your perspective on your struggles. Make a point to pray for your teen's struggle or challenge during the week and not just your own. If God shows you anything for your teen, share it with them.

Bible Story: Joseph's Journey (Genesis 37, 39-45)

Reflection: The story of Joseph is one of immense struggle, yet incredible trust in God. Betrayed by his brothers, sold into slavery, falsely accused, and imprisoned, Joseph could have easily given up hope. But he continued to trust God, even in the darkest moments. In the end, God used Joseph's trials to save many people, including his own family. Joseph's story reminds us that God is always working behind the scenes, using even our most difficult experiences for good. As adults, we often face struggles where it's hard to see God's purpose. Reflect on times when God brought good out of your challenges and consider how you can share this perspective with your teen.

Key Themes:

- Trusting God through betrayal, hardship, and uncertainty.

- Recognizing God's presence in the midst of trials.

- Understanding that God's plan is greater than the struggles we face.

Teen Devotional Recap:

- **Day 1:** *God is Present Even When Life is Hard* – Psalm 46:1 – God is our refuge and strength, always present to provide comfort and peace during difficult times.

- **Day 2:** *Stories of People Who Trusted God Through Trials (Job)* – Job 1:21 – Job's story reminds us to trust God even when we don't understand our suffering, knowing that He is still in control.

- **Day 3:** *How Difficulties Can Strengthen Your Faith* – James 1:2-3 – Trials and challenges are opportunities for growth, testing and strengthening our faith.

- **Day 4:** *The Importance of Holding Onto Hope* – Romans 15:13 – Hope in God anchors our faith, giving us peace and joy even in difficult circumstances.

- **Day 5:** *Practical Ways to Trust God During Struggles* – 1 Samuel 14:6 – There are practical ways to grow in trust during tough times, like praying, remembering God's faithfulness, and seeking support.

Weekly Summary:

This week focused on learning to trust God during difficult times. Your teen explored how God is present in our struggles, how trials can strengthen faith, and the importance of holding onto hope. Trusting God doesn't mean we have all the answers, but it means relying on His presence and promises. As a mentor, you can help your teen understand that God is faithful, even when life doesn't make sense, and that trusting Him brings peace and purpose.

Journaling Questions for Mentor:

1. How do you usually respond to difficult times in your life? How has trusting God through these times shaped your faith?

2. Reflect on the story of Job. How does his trust in God, even through suffering, encourage you in your own trials?

3. Think about a time when challenges in your life strengthened your faith. How can you share this experience with your teen to encourage them in their own struggles?

4. What promises of God give you hope during hard times? How can you help your teen anchor their faith in these promises?

5. What practical steps can you take this week to trust God more deeply in your own struggles? How can you model these steps for your teen?

Real-Life Story:

Joni Eareckson Tada: Finding Hope Amidst Suffering

Joni Eareckson Tada became a quadriplegic after a diving accident at the age of 17. Instead of allowing her suffering to consume her, she trusted God in the midst of her struggles. Joni learned to paint using her mouth, wrote books, and started a ministry to help others with disabilities. Reflecting back on her journey at one point, she said, "God's greatest blessings come through most unlikely and unexpected places, through pain and suffering" (Tada, 2010).

Her story is a testament to how God can use our pain for a greater purpose and how trust in Him can lead to hope and joy even in the hardest of times.

Discussion or Activity with Teen:

Activity:

Return to the persecuted church websites you visited in Week 4 and read some new testimonies that will encourage each of you to maintain your trust in God in difficult times, or if you have the Foxe's Book of Martyrs, you could read stories from there.

or

"Faith and Trust Journal"

1. **Identify Current Challenges:** Encourage your teen to write down any current struggles or worries they're facing. These can be big or small — anything that causes stress or uncertainty.

2. **Scripture Response:** For each challenge, ask them to write a Bible verse that speaks to God's faithfulness or strength (you can suggest verses like Isaiah 41:10, Psalm 46:1, or Romans 8:28 if they need help).

3. **Prayer of Trust:** Guide the teen to turn each challenge into a short prayer, thanking God for being with them and asking for trust in His plan.

Debrief: Discuss how it feels to acknowledge challenges while also choosing to trust in God's promises. Encourage them to keep returning to this journal when new struggles arise.

Conversation Starter:

"Trusting God When It's Hard"

Begin by sharing a time when you had to trust God in a situation where you didn't know the outcome. You can also bring the story of Joseph into the conversation if appropriate.

Then, ask your teen:

- "What is one challenge you're facing that makes it hard to trust God?"

- "How does knowing that God is with you, even in the hard times, help you feel differently about that challenge?"

- "What's one promise of God that you can hold onto when things don't make sense?"

This conversation can help them see that trust doesn't remove the struggle, but it changes how we experience it, offering peace and hope amid uncertainty.

WEEK 11

GOD'S PLAN FOR MY LIFE

Introduction:

This week, your teen will be learning about God's unique plan for their life. They will explore how to seek God's direction, trust His timing, and take small steps of obedience, even when His plan is unclear. Your role as a mentor is to encourage your teen to trust that God has a specific purpose for their life and to help them understand that following God's plan requires both patience and faith.

Practical Challenge:

Teen Challenge: Choose one decision you are facing and ask God to guide you in it. Spend time praying, reading Scripture, and listening for His direction. Trust that He will show you the next step, even if it's small.

Mentor Challenge: If you are facing a decision, join your teen in this challenge. Either way, be praying for your teen concerning their decision. Encourage your teen and at the end of the week, discuss how seeking God's guidance has helped you both make progress in understanding His plan. Remind your teen how important it is to worship the Lord during this time also and not just be seeking an answer, treating God like a genie.

Bible Story: God's Call to Abram (Genesis 12:1-9)

Reflection: In Genesis 12, God called Abram (later Abraham) to leave his home and go to a land that He would show him. Abram had no idea where this journey would take him, but he trusted God's plan and obeyed. Through Abram's obedience, God established His covenant and promised blessings not only for Abram but for the generations to come.

This story teaches us that God's plan often requires faith in the unknown, but it leads to blessings and fulfillment of His promises. As adults, we often face times when God's plan seems unclear. Reflect on how you've trusted God in uncertain times and how you can encourage your teen to do the same.

Key Themes:

- Trusting God's plan even when the destination is unknown.

- Taking small steps of faith and obedience.

- Recognizing that God's plan brings blessings and purpose.

Teen Devotional Recap:

- **Day 1:** *Understanding That God Has a Unique Plan for Each Person* – Jeremiah 29:11 – God has a specific plan for your life, one filled with hope, purpose, and good.

- **Day 2:** *Learning to Seek God's Direction Through Prayer and Scripture* – Psalm 32:8 – God promises to guide you and teach you through prayer and His Word.

- **Day 3:** *Patience in Waiting for God's Timing* – Psalm 27:14 – Waiting on God's timing can be difficult, but His timing is perfect, and waiting builds trust and maturity.

- **Day 4:** *Trusting God Even When His Plan is Unclear* – Psalm 37:5 – Trusting God means submitting to Him, even when His plan is unclear, and He promises to direct your path.

- **Day 5:** *Taking Small Steps of Obedience Toward God's Calling* – Micah 6:8 – God's plan often unfolds through small steps of obedience. Walk humbly and trust Him with each step.

Weekly Summary:

This week focused on God's unique plan for each person and how to seek His guidance through prayer and Scripture. Your teen learned the importance of patience in waiting for God's timing, trusting Him even when the plan is unclear, and taking small steps of obedience. As a mentor, your role is to help your teen understand that God's plan is personal and purposeful, and following His leading requires faith, patience, and trust.

Journaling Questions for Mentor:

1. How has trusting in God's unique plan for your life changed the way you approach decisions? Can you share a personal experience where God led you in an unexpected way?

2. Reflect on a time when seeking God's direction through prayer and Scripture helped you make a decision. How can you help your teen develop this practice?

3. In what areas of your life have you had to be patient for God's timing? How did trusting Him through that process strengthen your faith?

4. Think of a time when you didn't understand God's plan, but trusted Him anyway. How did it work out? How can you use this story to encourage your teen to trust God more deeply?

5. What small steps of obedience has God called you to take recently? How can you encourage your teen to trust God with each step, even if they don't know the full picture?

Real-Life Story:

Hudson Taylor: Trusting God's Plan in Missions

Hudson Taylor was a pioneering British missionary to China in the 1800s, a time in history when travel to China – especially inland China – was very difficult and dangerous. Keeping contact with the outside world and raising support from outside the country were nearly impossible. Taylor embraced his mission anyway, knowing that God had called him to inland China, and he ended up founding the China Inland Mission and brought the gospel to many who had never heard it.

One memorable story about Hudson Taylor involves his decision to adopt Chinese dress and shave his head in the style of Chinese men—a bold move that shocked many of his fellow missionaries and friends. Taylor felt strongly that he needed to identify with the local people to effectively share the gospel. This decision included wearing traditional Chinese clothing, which many Western missionaries found unnecessary and even undignified. Taylor's choice baffled those close to him; they thought he was going too far and didn't understand why he would abandon his own culture so completely. Yet, to Taylor, this was a step of faith and cultural respect. He believed that by dressing and living as the Chinese did, he could better connect with them and share the gospel in a way they could embrace. This approach later became a foundational practice in missions, emphasizing respect for local culture and adaptability. Taylor's trust in God's plan and willingness to obey, even when the path was unclear or didn't make sense, serve as inspiration for us to follow God wherever He leads (Taylor, 1997).

Discussion or Activity with Teen:

Activity:

If your teen has some idea about God's plan for their life, see if there is something practical you can do to help them investigate. For example many places will allow a teen to shadow an employee for the day to see what the job is like. If they are interested in missions, encourage them to investigate the options (e.g. Teen Missions Int'l, Global Year, YWAM, Experience Mission, etc.)

or

"My Path, God's Plan"

1. **Write a Dream or Goal List:** Encourage your teen to list a few dreams, goals, or hopes they have for their future — these can be related to school, personal interests, family, or career aspirations.

2. **Match with Scripture:** For each dream or goal, ask them to find a Bible verse that reflects trust, guidance, or God's plan (like Jeremiah 29:11, Proverbs 3:5-6, or Psalm 37:4).

3. **Pray Over Each Goal:** Lead them in a short prayer for each item, asking God to shape these desires according to His will and for patience in His timing.

Debrief: Discuss how it feels to offer their dreams to God. Talk about how seeking God's guidance isn't about giving up what matters to them, but about letting God guide them toward His best for their lives.

Conversation Starter:

"Trusting God's Plan Even When It's Unclear"

Begin by sharing a personal experience when you had to wait for God's plan to unfold or when His direction wasn't clear.

Then, ask your teen:

- "Is there something you're hoping or planning for, but you're not sure how it will work out?"

- "How can you seek God's guidance and trust Him, even if you don't know all the details yet?"

- "What's one small step of faith or obedience you can take toward that goal, trusting that God will guide the rest?"

This conversation can encourage them to see waiting as part of God's process and to take small steps with trust that He will lead.

WEEK 12

OBEYING GOD

Introduction:

This week, your teen will be learning about what it means to obey God in everyday life. They will explore how small acts of obedience lead to blessings, how to overcome challenges that make obedience difficult, and the importance of choosing God's way over the opinions of others. As a mentor, your role is to encourage your teen to walk in obedience and help them understand that obedience is an expression of love for God and trust in His plan.

Practical Challenge:

Teen Challenge: Identify one area in your life where you have struggled to obey God. Make a commitment to take one step of obedience this week, trusting that God will bless and strengthen you as you follow Him.

Mentor Challenge: (Same as the Teen Challenge) Encourage your teen and at the end of the week, discuss how obedience has impacted both of your walks with God. Try to recognize why it has been difficult to be obedient in that area of your life and notice if there are any underlying issues you need to deal with. Help the teen to do the same. It is always important to look at the roots of problems in our lives and not just the surface issues.

Bible Story: Jonah's Disobedience and Repentance (Jonah 1-3)

Reflection: In the book of Jonah, we see a clear example of the consequences of disobedience and the blessings of obedience. When God called Jonah to go to Nineveh, Jonah disobeyed and ran in the opposite direction. His disobedience led to a dangerous storm and time in the belly of a great fish. But after Jonah repented and obeyed God's call, he was used to bring the people of Nineveh to repentance. This story reminds us that while disobedience can have negative consequences, God is always ready to redirect us when we choose to obey. Reflect on how obedience to God's direction has shaped your life and how you can encourage your teen to trust and obey God, even when it's difficult.

Key Themes:

- The consequences of disobedience and the blessings of obedience.

- God's readiness to forgive and use us when we repent and obey.

- Trusting God's plan even when it challenges us.

Teen Devotional Recap:

- **Day 1:** *What Obedience Looks Like in Everyday Life* – John 14:15 – Obeying God is about making small, daily choices that honor Him and reflect His will in our lives.

- **Day 2:** *The Blessings That Come from Obedience* – Deuteronomy 28:1-2 – God promises blessings to those who obey, including peace, joy, and a deeper relationship with Him.

- **Day 3:** *Examples of Obedience in the Bible (Abraham)* – Genesis 12:1-2 – Abraham's obedience to God's call required faith and courage, and through his obedience, God fulfilled His greater plan.

- **Day 4:** *Overcoming Challenges That Make Obedience Difficult* – Galatians 5:16 – Obedience can be hard, but the Holy Spirit helps us overcome temptations and distractions, guiding us to follow God's commands.

- **Day 5:** *Choosing Obedience Over the Opinions of Others* – Acts 5:29 – When obeying God conflicts with the opinions of others, we must remember that obedience to God brings lasting rewards and honors Him above all.

Weekly Summary:

This week focused on what obedience looks like in daily life and the blessings that come from it. The teen learned from biblical examples like Abraham, who trusted and obeyed God despite uncertainty. They also explored how to overcome challenges to obedience and how to prioritize God's way over the opinions of others. As a mentor, your role is to help your teen see that obedience is about living a life that honors God and walking in His will, even when it's difficult.

Journaling Questions for Mentor:

1. What small acts of obedience do you practice in your daily life? How have they strengthened your relationship with God?

2. Reflect on a time when obeying God brought unexpected blessings. How can you share this story with your teen to encourage them in their obedience?

3. In what ways do you find it challenging to obey God in certain areas of your life? How do you rely on the Holy Spirit to help you overcome these challenges?

4. How do you handle situations where obeying God conflicts with the opinions of others? What can you learn from the example of the apostles in Acts 5:29?

5. How can you encourage your teen to take small steps of obedience, trusting that God will bless and strengthen them as they follow Him?

Real-Life Story:

David Wilkerson: A Call to Obedience in Ministry

David Wilkerson was an American pastor who felt God calling him to reach out to troubled gang members and drug addicts in New York City in the 1950s. In one notable encounter, Wilkerson approached Nicky Cruz, a notorious gang leader of the feared gang, the Mau Maus. Cruz, who had lived a life filled with violence and anger, threatened Wilkerson and told him he would kill him if he didn't leave. Undeterred, Wilkerson famously responded, "You could cut me into a thousand pieces and lay them in the street, and every piece would still love you."

Wilkerson's courage, faith, and love were disarming. Despite the real danger, he continued to reach out to Cruz and other gang members with God's message of forgiveness and redemption. Over time, his persistence broke through to Cruz, who eventually gave his life to Christ. This encounter marked the beginning of Wilkerson's ministry, Teen Challenge, which went on to help thousands of gang members, drug addicts, and troubled youth find freedom from addiction and hope in Christ. His obedience to God's leading led to countless transformed lives and demonstrates how powerful obedience can be when we listen and respond to God's voice (Wilkerson, 1963).

Discussion or Activity with Teen:

Activity:

Give your teen a plant with the instructions of how to care for it. Let the plant care be a reminder of our obedience to God. A few days of distraction can kill the plant just like a few days of distraction and disobedience can harm our walk with God. Diligent obedience, though, can cause the plant and us to flourish and grow.

or

"Obedience Steps"

1. **Choose a Small Act of Obedience:** Ask your teen to think of one area in their life where they can practice obedience to God for the next month. This could be honoring their parents, speaking kindly, spending time in prayer, or any area where they feel God nudging them.

2. **Write It Down:** Have them write down the act of obedience on a note card, along with a related Bible verse (like 1 Samuel 15:22, "To obey is better than sacrifice...") and place it somewhere where they will see it daily.

3. **Follow Through and Reflect:** Encourage them to follow through with this act during the month. At the end, they can reflect on how it felt to choose obedience and any blessings or peace they experienced from honoring God in this way.

Debrief: (Put the date for one month from now in your calendar so that you don't forget.) Talk about how small steps of obedience prepare us for greater acts of obedience and strengthen our faith in God's guidance.

Conversation Starter:

"Why Obedience Matters"

Begin by sharing a story of a time when you had to choose obedience, even though it was difficult or went against popular opinion.

Then, ask your teen:

- "What's an example of a time when you had to choose obedience to God over what others thought or wanted?"

- "What do you think God is asking of you right now that might require a step of obedience?"

- "What can help you stay committed to obedience when it's challenging?"

This conversation can help your teen see obedience as a personal journey of faith and a way to experience God's presence and blessings in their life.

WEEK 13

DEVELOPING SPIRITUAL HABITS

Introduction:

This week, your teen will be learning about the importance of developing spiritual habits like Bible reading, prayer, worship, fasting, and accountability. These practices are essential for spiritual growth and staying connected to God's truth. As a mentor, your role is to help your teen understand how these habits strengthen their relationship with God and to encourage them to be consistent in practicing them.

Practical Challenge:

Teen Challenge: Choose one spiritual habit to focus on this week. Whether it's setting aside time to read the Bible, praying daily, worshiping intentionally, fasting for a meal, or finding an accountability partner, make it a goal to be consistent with that habit and see how it helps you grow.

Mentor Challenge: (Same as the Teen Challenge) Be sure to pick a new spiritual habit or perhaps increase the time or frequency of an existing habit. Encourage your teen and at the end of the week discuss how these habits have strengthened your relationship with God.

Bible Story: Daniel's Commitment to Spiritual Habits (Daniel 1-2)

Reflection: In Daniel 1-2, we see Daniel's commitment to his faith and spiritual habits from the start of his time in Babylon. Despite being in a foreign land, Daniel refused to compromise his beliefs. In Daniel 1, he chose to follow a strict diet based on God's laws rather than indulging in the royal food and drink. Later, in Daniel 2, Daniel prayed earnestly for God to reveal King Nebuchadnezzar's dream, showing his dependence on God's guidance. These stories highlight the power of spiritual habits in sustaining faith and receiving God's wisdom, even in challenging circumstances. Daniel's commitment to prayer, obedience, and discipline not only strengthened his own faith but also influenced those around him.

Key Themes:

- Commitment to spiritual habits like prayer and obedience, even in difficult situations.

- How spiritual disciplines strengthen our faith and provide wisdom.

- The impact of staying faithful to God's Word and His guidance.

Teen Devotional Recap:

- **Day 1:** *The Importance of Daily Bible Reading* – Matthew 4:4 – Developing the habit of reading the Bible daily helps nourish our spirits and gives us wisdom and guidance for life.

- **Day 2:** *Setting Aside Time for Solitude and Silence* – Mark 1:35 – Just as Jesus made time for solitude, we are called to set aside intentional time to pray, reflect, and listen, in order to grow closer to God.

- **Day 3:** Gratitude *as a Regular Part of Your Week* – Hebrews 13:15 – Being thankful shifts our perspective. It causes us to remember God's goodness and all that He has done for us and in us.

- **Day 4:** *Fasting and Other Spiritual Disciplines* – Matthew 6:17-18 – Fasting and other disciplines like solitude and silence help us draw closer to God, seek Him with intensity, and grow in spiritual maturity.

- **Day 5:** *Developing Accountability in Your Spiritual Walk* – Ecclesiastes 4:9-10 – Accountability partners help keep us on track in our faith, encouraging us and challenging us to grow in our spiritual habits.

Weekly Summary:

This week focused on the importance of developing spiritual habits like Bible reading, prayer, worship, fasting, and accountability. These practices draw us closer to God, deepen our faith, and help us stay grounded in His truth. Your teen explored how spiritual habits help us grow in our relationship with God and how consistency in these practices leads to greater spiritual maturity.

Journaling Questions for Mentor:

1. What spiritual habits have helped you grow in your relationship with God? How can you encourage your teen to develop similar habits?

2. Reflect on a time when setting aside time for prayer and Bible reading made a significant difference in your life. How can you share this experience to encourage your teen?

3. How has worship — whether through singing, serving, or another form — impacted your relationship with God? How can you explain this to your teen in a way that helps them see the importance of worship?

4. What spiritual discipline, like fasting or solitude, has helped you grow closer to God? How can you encourage your teen to try a new spiritual discipline?

5. Who has been an accountability partner in your spiritual journey? How can you help your teen find someone (in addition to you) to encourage and challenge them in their faith?

Real-Life Story:

Billy Graham: A Life of Spiritual Discipline

Billy Graham, one of the most well-known evangelists in history, was known for his commitment to spiritual habits. He read the Bible daily, spent intentional time in prayer, and prioritized sharing his faith. His disciplined spiritual life enabled him to impact millions of people worldwide with the message of Jesus. As he became more and more successful as an evangelist, he never lost sight of his need to practice spiritual disciplines every day in order to keep his focus on the Lord and his heart in the right place. He once said, "If you don't feel close to God, guess who moved? Discipline yourself to find time each day to talk to God, study His Word, and listen for His voice" (Graham, 2006).

Graham's example reminds us that consistent spiritual habits not only grow our faith but also empower us to share God's love with others.

Discussion or Activity with Teen:

Activity:

Plan a day to fast together with your teen. Choose a God-centered focus for your prayers that day, such as asking God to teach you to love Him more. Remember that God focuses on the process as much as the result. This is seen in all the agricultural parables of Jesus. Do not expect instant results, but expect to see a process beginning.

or

"Spiritual Habit Tracker"

1. Create a Habit Tracker: Have your teen create a simple monthly habit tracker for spiritual practices like Bible reading, prayer, worship, and any other habit they feel drawn to start or deepen. They can use a journal or make a simple chart with each day of the week.

2. Set Small, Achievable Goals: Encourage them to set small, achievable goals, like reading one Bible verse each day, praying for five minutes, or spending a few minutes in worship. Consistency is key, so keeping goals manageable helps build the habit.

3. Reflect on the month: At the end of the month (set a reminder in your calendar), ask them to reflect on how these practices impacted their daily life. Did they notice any growth in their relationship with God or feel a greater sense of peace?

Debrief: Discuss how consistent habits, even if they start small, lead to spiritual growth and help keep us connected to God in everyday life.

Conversation Starter:

"Building a Habit of Faith"

Begin by sharing a spiritual habit that has been meaningful to you and how it's helped you grow closer to God over time. Also share an area that you know you need to improve, demonstrating to your teen that this is a life-long journey.

Then, ask your teen:

- "Which spiritual habit do you feel most excited to build or strengthen, and why?"

- "What do you think might make it difficult to stay consistent, and how could you work through those challenges?"

- "What's one way you've felt closer to God recently, and how can a spiritual habit help you keep growing that connection?"

This conversation can help your teen see spiritual habits as more than routine, but as intentional practices that shape their faith and help them experience God's presence consistently.

WEEK 14

DEALING WITH DOUBTS

Introduction:

This week, your teen will be learning about how to deal with doubts in their faith. They will explore how doubts are a normal part of faith, how to seek answers to their questions, and the importance of trusting God even when they don't have all the answers. Your role as a mentor is to encourage your teen to bring their doubts to God and to remind them that seeking truth can lead to a stronger and deeper faith.

Practical Challenge:

Teen Challenge: Write down one of your current doubts or questions about God or faith. Spend time praying about it, searching the Bible for answers, and talking to a trusted friend or mentor. Ask God to strengthen your faith as you seek Him.

Mentor Challenge: Encourage your teen and at the end of the week, discuss how seeking answers has impacted your faith and trust in God. Be sure to not bring any guilt or condemnation to your teen for whatever doubts or questions they might have. Even if you feel like you have the answer, let your teen spend the week seeking God. If at the end of the week they have not received revelation from God, then share what God has taught you about their area of doubt.

Bible Story: Thomas and His Doubts (John 20:24-29)

Reflection: In John 20, Thomas, one of Jesus' disciples, expressed doubt when the other disciples told him they had seen the risen Lord. He famously declared, "Unless I see the nail marks in His hands and put my finger where the nails were, and put my hand into

His side, I will not believe." When Jesus appeared to Thomas and invited him to touch His wounds, Thomas's doubts were replaced with faith, and he declared, "My Lord and my God!" Jesus responded by blessing those who believe without seeing. Thomas's story reminds us that doubts don't disqualify us from faith — they are opportunities to seek truth and grow in understanding. Jesus is patient with our doubts and invites us to trust Him, even when we can't see the full picture.

Key Themes:

- Doubts are normal and do not mean a lack of faith.

- Jesus is patient with our doubts and invites us to seek Him.

- Faith can grow stronger when we bring our doubts to God.

Teen Devotional Recap:

- **Day 1:** *Doubts are a Normal Part of Faith* – Mark 9:24 – Doubts don't mean our faith is weak. Everyone has questions at times, and we can bring those doubts to God.

- **Day 2:** *How to Seek Answers to Your Questions* – Jeremiah 33:3 – God promises to reveal truth to those who genuinely seek Him. We can find answers to our doubts through prayer, Scripture, and trusted mentors.

- **Day 3:** *Trusting God Even When You Don't Have All the Answers* – Isaiah 26:3 – Faith involves trusting God's wisdom and goodness, even when we don't understand everything.

- **Day 4:** *Finding Reassurance in God's Promises* – Deuteronomy 31:8 – God's promises give us reassurance in times of doubt. He promises to be with us, to strengthen us, and to uphold us.

- **Day 5:** *Surrounding Yourself with People Who Encourage Your Faith* – Hebrews 12:1 – Having a community of believers around us can strengthen our faith when we face doubts. It's important to seek support from friends who encourage us.

Weekly Summary:

This week focused on how doubts are a normal part of faith and can lead to deeper understanding when we seek God's answers. Your teen learned the importance of trusting God even when they don't have all the answers and finding reassurance in His promises.

Surrounding themselves with people who encourage their faith helps them stay strong in their relationship with God. As a mentor, your role is to remind your teen that doubts don't have to weaken their faith — they can actually strengthen it when they bring them to God.

Journaling Questions for Mentor:

1. What doubts or questions about your faith have you experienced in the past? How did you seek answers to those questions, and how did it impact your relationship with God?

2. Reflect on a time when you had to trust God even when you didn't have all the answers. How can you share this experience with your teen to encourage them in their own journey?

3. How do you find reassurance in God's promises during times of doubt? How can you help your teen anchor their faith in God's Word during times of uncertainty?

4. Who are the people in your life who encourage your faith? How can you help your teen build a support network of people who will strengthen and encourage them in their walk with God?

5. How can you model openness about your doubts and questions with your teen, showing them that it's okay to ask questions and seek truth?

Real-Life Story:

C.S. Lewis: From Atheism to Faith

C.S. Lewis, the famous author of *The Chronicles of Narnia*, was once an atheist who had many doubts about God and Christianity. However, he also highly valued truth and sought it out fervently. For a long time, he devoted himself to intense study and research in an effort to prove once-and-for-all that Christianity could not be true. In recalling the culmination of all his research and efforts, Lewis says:

"You must picture me alone in that room in Magdalen, night after night, feeling, whenever my mind lifted even for a second from my work, the steady, unrelenting approach of Him whom I so earnestly desired not to meet. That which I greatly feared had at last come upon me. I gave in, and admitted that God was God, and knelt and prayed: perhaps, that night, the most dejected and reluctant convert in all England" (Lewis, 1955).

Lewis struggled deeply with doubts and resisted belief in God for many years. However, his relentless search for truth eventually led him to a place where he could no longer deny God's presence, marking the beginning of his Christian journey. Through seeking truth, reading Scripture, and talking with friends like J.R.R. Tolkien, Lewis eventually came not only to believe in God, but also to be a strong defender of the Christian faith. His journey shows that doubts can lead to deeper faith when we seek the Truth with open hearts and minds.

Discussion or Activity with Teen:

Activity:

Watch or read *The Case for Christ* by Lee Strobel together. Discuss the questions that Lee struggles with and the answers he discovered, especially those that relate to your teen's questions. We can find encouragement in the testimony of others who have walked this road before us.

or

"Doubt to Discovery Journal"

1. **Write Down Doubts or Questions:** Encourage your teen to create a "Doubt to Discovery" page in their journal where they can honestly write down any doubts, questions, or uncertainties about their faith or God's promises.

2. **Find Scriptures or Promises:** Ask them to search for Bible verses or promises that address each doubt or question. You can support by suggesting verses or helping them look them up.

3. **Reflection on Growth:** Each week, have them review their entries and reflect on whether they've gained new insight, experienced peace, or found answers through prayer, reading, or talking to others. Seeing how God meets them in their questions can strengthen their trust in Him.

Debrief: After a few entries, discuss how addressing doubts in this way helps to turn questions into learning moments that build faith.

Conversation Starter:

"Turning Questions into Growth"

Start by sharing a time when you had a question or doubt about your faith and how God helped you understand or find peace in it. During your conversation it may be appropriate to discuss the difference between God, the Creator of the universe, and a genie that just comes to meet our demands and then we put him back in the bottle. Often our confusion about God has to do with our lack of understanding who He is. It's important to remember that building relationship and building our character are very high priorities for God.

Then, ask your teen:

- "What's one question you have about faith or God that you'd like to understand better?"

- "How do you feel about bringing your doubts or questions to God in prayer? Does it help you feel closer to Him?"

- "Who in your life helps encourage your faith when you have doubts? How do they support you?"

This conversation can help them see that doubt doesn't need to be feared but can be a way to build a stronger, more resilient faith.

WEEK 15

THE ROLE OF THE HOLY SPIRIT

Introduction:

This week, your teen will be learning about the role of the Holy Spirit in their life. They will explore who the Holy Spirit is, how He guides and comforts us, and the fruits that He produces in our lives. Your role as a mentor is to encourage your teen to rely on the Holy Spirit for guidance, strength, and growth in their faith. Help them understand that the Holy Spirit's presence is essential for living a life that honors God.

Practical Challenge:

Teen Challenge: **Pray each day this week for the Holy Spirit to fill and guide you.** Spend a few moments asking God to help you grow in the fruits of the Spirit and to rely on His strength in all that you do. Watch how God's Spirit works in your heart and actions.

Mentor Challenge: (Same as the Teen Challenge) We all need to be filled afresh with the Holy Spirit, and there is always room for growth in the fruits of the Spirit. Encourage your teen and, at the end of the week, discuss how being led by the Holy Spirit has impacted your faith and actions.

Bible Story: The Day of Pentecost (Acts 2:1-4)

Reflection: In Acts 2, we read about the incredible moment when the Holy Spirit was poured out on the believers at Pentecost. This event marked the beginning of the disciples' powerful ministry, as they were filled with the Holy Spirit and began to speak in different languages, boldly proclaiming the gospel. The Holy Spirit transformed these ordinary men into bold witnesses for Christ, empowering them to do what they could not do in their own strength. The Day of Pentecost shows us that the Holy Spirit equips us for God's work and enables us to live out our faith in ways that bring glory to God. As adults, we understand the importance of relying on the Holy Spirit daily, and we can encourage our teen to do the same as they grow in their walk with Christ.

Key Themes:

- The power of the Holy Spirit to transform and equip believers for God's work.

- How the Holy Spirit enables us to boldly live out our faith.

- The importance of being filled with the Holy Spirit and relying on His strength.

Teen Devotional Recap:

- **Day 1:** *Who the Holy Spirit Is* – John 14:26 – The Holy Spirit is God's presence within us, guiding, teaching, and comforting us as we walk with God.

- **Day 2:** *How the Holy Spirit Guides and Comforts Us* – Romans 8:14 – The Holy Spirit actively leads and comforts us in our daily lives, helping us stay close to God's will.

- **Day 3:** *The Fruits of the Spirit* – Galatians 5:22-23 – When we live by the Holy Spirit, our lives produce the fruit of God's character: love, joy, peace, patience, kindness, goodness, faithfulness, gentleness, and self-control.

- **Day 4:** *How to Be Filled with the Holy Spirit* – Ephesians 5:18 – Being filled with the Holy Spirit means surrendering our lives to His control and allowing Him to empower our actions.

- **Day 5:** *Relying on the Holy Spirit for Daily Strength* – Zechariah 4:6 – We cannot live a life that honors God in our own strength; we need the power of the Holy Spirit to give us wisdom, strength, and courage.

Weekly Summary:

This week focused on the role of the Holy Spirit as our guide, teacher, and source of strength. Your teen learned about the fruits of the Spirit and how being filled with the Holy Spirit enables them to live in a way that reflects God's character. They also explored how relying on the Holy Spirit daily equips them to navigate life's challenges and grow in their faith. As a mentor, your role is to help your teen understand that the Holy Spirit is essential to living a victorious Christian life.

Journaling Questions for Mentor:

1. How has the Holy Spirit guided or comforted you in your own life? How can you share this experience with your teen to help them understand the role of the Holy Spirit?

2. Reflect on a time when you experienced the fruits of the Spirit in your life. Which fruit of the Spirit do you feel God is calling you to grow in more, and how can you encourage your teen to focus on these fruits as well?

3. What does it look like in your life to be filled with the Holy Spirit? How can you help your teen understand what it means to surrender to the Holy Spirit's influence?

4. How do you rely on the Holy Spirit for strength in your daily life? How can you model this reliance for your teen, especially in challenging situations?

5. How can you encourage your teen to pray for the Holy Spirit's guidance and strength as they face decisions, challenges, and opportunities to grow in their faith?

Real-Life Story:

Smith Wigglesworth: A Life Transformed by the Holy Spirit

Smith Wigglesworth, a British evangelist in the early 20th century, was known for his passionate faith and reliance on the Holy Spirit. But he wasn't always confident in his faith. His early life was marked by his focus on his career as a plumber, periods of struggling with doubt, and a lack of desire to grow in his faith. But when he accepted a friend's invitation to a meeting where an evangelist was preaching, he was stirred with a strong desire to have a deeper relationship with the Lord. He requested prayer to be baptized in the Holy Spirit, and his life was transformed. He began preaching, praying for miraculous healings for others, and boldly sharing the Gospel around the world. The Holy Spirit empowers ordinary people to do extraordinary things for God (Wigglesworth, 2002).

Discussion or Activity with Teen:

Activity:

Read Acts 1:8, Acts 2:1-4, Acts 4:28-31, Acts 8:15-17, Acts 10:44 and Acts 19:6 together and discuss the importance that the early church placed on "being filled with the Spirit" and how that might apply to each of your lives. Then pray together for a fresh filling of the Holy Spirit.

or

"Fruit of the Spirit Challenge"

1. **List the Fruits:** Start by reviewing the fruits of the Spirit in Galatians 5:22-23 (love, joy, peace, patience, kindness, goodness, faithfulness, gentleness, and self-control).

2. **Daily Focus:** Ask your teen to pick one fruit each day to focus on and pray for guidance from the Holy Spirit in showing that quality. For example, if they choose patience, they might ask the Holy Spirit to help them respond patiently in situations that usually frustrate them.

3. **Reflection:** At the end of each day, have them reflect on how the Holy Spirit helped them live out that particular fruit. They can journal about any challenges they faced or moments where they felt the Spirit's guidance or strength.

Debrief: At the end of the week, discuss together which fruits were the easiest or hardest to display and how the Holy Spirit's presence made a difference.

Conversation Starter:

"Living with the Spirit's Guidance"

Begin by sharing an example of a time when you felt the Holy Spirit guiding or strengthening you in a challenging situation.

Then, ask your teen:

- "What's one area of your life where you think you could really use the Holy Spirit's help right now?"

- "When you're facing something difficult, how often do you remember to ask the Holy Spirit for guidance or strength?"

- "Which of the fruits of the Spirit do you think others see most clearly in you? Are there any you'd like to grow in?"

This conversation can encourage your teen to rely on the Holy Spirit more intentionally and recognize His role in their growth and daily life.

WEEK 16

GOD'S GRACE AND FORGIVENESS

Introduction:

This week, your teen will be learning about God's grace and forgiveness. They will explore what grace means as an unearned gift, why we need God's forgiveness, and how to live in the freedom that comes from being forgiven. As a mentor, your role is to help your teen understand the depth of God's grace and to encourage them to extend that grace to themselves and others. Help them reflect on how forgiveness brings freedom and restores relationships.

Practical Challenge:

Teen Challenge: Take time this week to reflect on God's grace and forgiveness. If there is an area where you need to forgive yourself or someone else, ask God to help you take that step. Write down a verse about grace to carry with you and remind yourself of God's unconditional love and forgiveness.

Mentor Challenge: (Same as the Teen Challenge) Encourage your teen and at the end of the week, discuss how embracing God's grace has impacted your hearts and relationships.

Bible Story: Jonah's Restoration and Nineveh's Forgiveness (Jonah 1-4)

Reflection: The story of Jonah beautifully illustrates God's eagerness to forgive and restore, even when we run from Him or fail. Jonah's disobedience in fleeing from God's call (Jonah 1:3) led to a storm and his being swallowed by a great fish, yet God mercifully gave him a second chance. In Jonah 2:2, Jonah cries out, "In my distress I called to the Lord, and He answered me," showing how God hears and responds to genuine repentance. Later, despite the wickedness of Nineveh, God's compassion shines through as He relents from destroying the city when they turn from their evil ways (Jonah 3:10). This story reminds us that no failure is too great for God's mercy and that His heart longs to restore us when we return to Him.

Key Themes:

- The grace of God to forgive us even when we fail or are disobedient.

- The power of restoration and second chances.

- How God's grace empowers us to continue serving Him after failure.

Teen Devotional Recap:

- **Day 1:** *Understanding Grace as a Gift from God* – Ephesians 2:8-9 – Grace is God's unearned favor, given freely to those who believe. It's not something we can earn; it's a gift.

- **Day 2:** *Why We Need God's Forgiveness* – Romans 3:23-24 – All have sinned and fallen short of God's perfect standard, but God offers forgiveness through Jesus to bridge that gap.

- **Day 3:** *How to Accept God's Grace and Forgive Ourselves* – 1 John 1:9 – Confessing our sins allows us to receive God's forgiveness. Accepting His grace also involves forgiving ourselves.

- **Day 4:** *Offering Grace and Forgiveness to Others* – Colossians 3:13 – Just as God has forgiven us, we are called to forgive others, reflecting God's grace in our relationships.

- **Day 5:** *Living in Freedom Because of God's Grace* – Romans 8:1 – There is no condemnation for those who are in Christ. God's grace frees us from guilt and empowers us to live in His love.

Weekly Summary:

This week focused on God's grace and forgiveness. Your teen learned that grace is a gift from God, not something we earn, and that we all need forgiveness because of our sin. They explored how to accept God's grace, forgive themselves, and extend forgiveness to others. Living in grace means walking in the freedom that comes from knowing there is no condemnation in Christ. As a mentor, help your teen understand how embracing God's grace transforms their relationships and allows them to live in freedom and love.

Journaling Questions for Mentor:

1. How have you experienced God's grace in your life, and how has it changed the way you view yourself and your relationship with God?

2. Reflect on a time when you found it difficult to forgive yourself. How did you come to accept God's grace and let go of shame?

3. How do you approach offering forgiveness to others when you've been hurt? What has helped you extend grace in difficult situations?

4. What does living in the freedom of God's grace look like in your daily life? How can you encourage your teen to walk in that same freedom?

5. How can you model forgiveness in your relationships, showing your teen what it means to reflect God's grace to others?

Real-Life Story:

John Newton: The Man Behind "Amazing Grace"

John Newton's journey to Christianity was as dramatic as it was transformative. Newton, a former slave ship captain, was known for his reckless and profane life. However, one night in 1748, while sailing through a violent storm off the coast of Ireland, he faced what he thought would be certain death. As the storm raged and water flooded the ship, Newton cried out, "Lord, have mercy on us!"

Miraculously, the ship survived, and Newton was left shaken and introspective. That night marked a turning point. Newton began to study the Bible and reflect on his life, eventually embracing Christianity. Over time, his faith grew, and he completely renounced the slave trade, later becoming a pastor and a prominent abolitionist. He would go on to write the famous hymn "Amazing Grace," which beautifully captured his story of redemption: *"I once was lost, but now am found; was blind, but now I see"* (Newton, 2003).

Newton's story reminds us that no matter our past, God's grace is available to all, offering new life and freedom.

Discussion or Activity with Teen:

Activity:

If your teen is aware of a very specific person they need to forgive (even themselves) encourage them to be obedient and forgive. Help them decide if that needs to be a prayer, a declaration, a phone call, a personal encounter with someone, or some combination. Remind them that it is not about an emotional feeling, but a rational decision to agree with God. It might take some time for the emotions to change and agree with that decision.

or

"Grace and Forgiveness Reflection"

1. **Reflect on Grace and Forgiveness**: Have the teen write down or draw two large circles that overlap slightly: one labeled "God's Grace" and the other "Forgiveness for Others." In the overlap write "ME"

2. **Self-Reflection on Grace**: In the "God's Grace" circle, ask them to write about times when they felt unworthy but experienced God's love and grace. Encourage them to reflect on how those moments impacted their view of God's forgiveness.

3. **Forgiving Others**: In the "Forgiveness for Others" circle, ask them to consider anyone they may need to forgive. Have them write down any feelings or struggles they have with forgiveness. Encourage them to pray, asking God for the strength to extend forgiveness, just as He has forgiven them. Help them recognize that they are the middle step of transmitting God's forgiveness to others.

Debrief: Discuss how recognizing God's grace for them makes it easier (or more challenging) to forgive others. Talk about any changes they'd like to make to live more fully in grace.

Conversation Starter:

"Embracing and Extending Grace"

Begin by sharing a story of a time when you struggled to accept grace or forgive someone and how God helped you through it.

Then, ask your teen:

- "When you think about God's grace, what's the first thing that comes to mind?

Do you find it easy or difficult to believe that God forgives you fully?"

- "Is there someone you've struggled to forgive? How might seeing them through God's eyes — as a person who also needs grace — change your perspective?"

- "How do you think embracing God's grace might change the way you view yourself and others?"

This conversation can help your teen see grace and forgiveness as freeing, both in their own life and in their relationships with others.

WEEK 17

EXPERIENCING GOD'S PRESENCE

Introduction:

This week, your teen will be learning about how to experience God's presence in their lives. They will explore how God's presence can be felt in quiet moments, in community, and even in times when we don't feel Him. Your role as a mentor is to encourage your teen to recognize God's presence in every season and to trust that He is always near, even when life feels difficult or uncertain. Help them learn how to cultivate an awareness of God's presence that brings peace and comfort.

Practical Challenge:

Teen Challenge: Spend 10 minutes each day this week in quiet reflection or prayer. Turn off distractions and focus on being still before God. Ask Him to reveal His presence to you and to fill your heart with His peace.

Mentor Challenge: (Same as the Teen Challenge) Apart from your usual routine, find 10 minutes to just be still before the Lord, meditating on Him and His goodness. Encourage your teen and, at the end of the week, discuss how experiencing God's presence has impacted your thoughts, emotions, and sense of peace.

Bible Story: Peter Walking on Water and Jesus' Presence (Matthew 14:22-33)

Reflection: In Matthew 14, we see a powerful example of God's presence through the story of Peter walking on water. As the disciples struggled against the wind and waves, they saw Jesus walking toward them on the water. Peter, filled with faith, asked Jesus to command him to walk on the water as well. Jesus invited Peter to come, and Peter walked on the water toward Jesus. But when Peter took his eyes off Jesus and focused on the storm around him, he began to sink. Immediately, Jesus reached out His hand and caught Peter. This story illustrates that God's presence is with us, even in the midst of life's storms. When we fix our eyes on Jesus, we can trust that He will guide us, sustain us, and provide peace. Even when we feel overwhelmed, God's presence is constant, and He is ready to reach out and rescue us when we call.

Key Themes:

- Experiencing God's presence in both quiet moments and life's storms.

- The importance of keeping our focus on Jesus to experience peace.

- Trusting in God's presence, even when fear or doubt arises.

Teen Devotional Recap:

- **Day 1:** *Recognizing God's Presence in Quiet Moments* – Psalm 46:10 – God often speaks to us in quiet moments. Being still before God allows us to hear His voice and feel His presence.

- **Day 2:** *Feeling God's Presence in Community and Worship* – Matthew 18:20 – God's presence is not just experienced alone but also in community. Worship with others allows us to experience the joy and encouragement of God's presence together.

- **Day 3:** *Trusting That God is With You Even When You Don't Feel Him* – Joshua 1:9 – Even when we don't feel God's presence, He promises to be with us always. Trusting in His presence strengthens us during difficult times.

- **Day 4:** *How to Cultivate a Sense of God's Presence* – James 4:8 – Drawing near to God through prayer, worship, and Scripture cultivates an awareness of His presence. God desires to be close to us and promises to draw near when we seek Him.

- **Day 5:** *The Peace That Comes from Knowing God is Always Near* – Philippians 4:7 – God's presence brings peace that surpasses all understanding. Knowing He is always near gives us a calm assurance, even in life's storms.

Weekly Summary:

This week focused on experiencing God's presence in quiet moments, in community, and in every season of life. Your teen learned that even when they don't feel God's presence, they can trust that He is always near. They explored how cultivating an awareness of God's presence through prayer, worship, and Scripture brings peace and joy. As a mentor, encourage your teen to trust in God's constant presence and help them recognize how God is with them in both the good and challenging times.

Journaling Questions for Mentor:

1. How have you experienced God's presence in both quiet moments and difficult times? How can you share this experience with your teen to encourage them in their own walk?

2. Reflect on a time when you felt God's presence in a community of believers or during worship. How did this experience strengthen your faith?

3. How do you respond when you don't feel God's presence? What helps you trust that He is still with you even in those moments?

4. What practices (prayer, Scripture reading, worship) help you cultivate an awareness of God's presence in your daily life? How can you encourage your teen to develop similar habits?

5. How can you model a life that is centered on God's presence, offering peace and assurance to those around you, especially your teen?

Real-Life Story:

Brother Andrew: Practicing God's Presence in Dangerous Situations

Brother Andrew, also known as "God's Smuggler," risked his life to bring Bibles to Christians in countries where the gospel was forbidden. Even when facing danger, he trusted in God's presence and protection. He would often pray, "Lord, in my luggage I have Scripture that I want to take to Your children. When You were on earth, You made blind eyes see. Now I pray, make seeing eyes blind" (Brother Andrew, 1967).

He has many incredible stories of seeing God intervene in just the right way at just the right moment in his situation so that his life was preserved, and he was able to carry out his mission of bringing the Word of God to isolated believers in closed-off countries. His faith and sense of God's presence with him always empowered him to share God's Word despite the risks.

Discussion or Activity with Teen:

Activity:

Jesus often spent time in nature to be in the presence of the Father. Take your teen to a quiet place in nature and meditate together on God's greatness. Remember the use of ACTS prayer, your discussions about worship, God's forgiveness given to each of you through Jesus' sacrifice, and anything else the Holy Spirit brings to remembrance from your journey together thus far. Let the time be mixed with stillness/silence, testimony, praise, worship, and awe. In any supplication or requests, continue to ask to be filled afresh with the Holy Spirit.

or

"Presence Journal"

1. **Daily Presence Log**: Give the teen a notebook or sheet of paper where they can jot down moments throughout each day when they sense or remember God's presence. Encourage them to include small things — like a moment of peace, something beautiful in nature, or an answered prayer — as well as any challenges where they needed extra reassurance of God's presence.

2. **Reflection Time**: At the end of the week, have them look back at their notes. Ask them to think about how God showed up in their daily life, even in unexpected ways.

Debrief: Discuss what surprised them, encouraged them, or gave them peace as they looked back on these moments. Ask them to consider how keeping track of God's presence might change their awareness moving forward.

Conversation Starter:

"Recognizing God's Presence"

Start with a story of a time you felt God's presence in a difficult moment or a quiet time.

Then, ask your teen:

- "When are you most aware of God's presence? Is it easier to feel Him close during good times or challenging times?"

- "Have there been moments this week when you sensed God was with you, even if it wasn't obvious right away?"

- "How does knowing God is always with you change the way you approach everyday situations or challenges?"

This conversation can help your teen see that God's presence isn't based on feelings but on His promise to be with them always, giving peace and joy through every season.

WEEK 18

SHARING YOUR FAITH

Introduction:

This week, your teen will be learning about the importance of sharing their faith. They will explore why evangelism matters, how to share their testimony, and how to overcome fear when talking about Jesus. Your role as a mentor is to encourage your teen to see sharing their faith as a natural outpouring of their relationship with God. Help them understand that evangelism is not about having all the right answers but about showing love and letting God use their words and actions to impact others.

Practical Challenge:

Teen Challenge: Choose one person this week to intentionally share your faith with. Whether it's through telling your story, offering to pray for them, or simply showing kindness, look for an opportunity to reflect God's love and make Him known.

Mentor Challenge: (Same as the Teen Challenge) Encourage your teen and, at the end of the week, discuss how God worked through both of your conversations and actions to touch others.

Bible Story: Philip and the Ethiopian Eunuch (Acts 8:26-40)

Reflection: In Acts 8, we find the story of Philip, who was led by the Holy Spirit to share the gospel with an Ethiopian official. As Philip approached the man, he heard him reading from the book of Isaiah but not fully understanding the meaning. Philip asked the man if he understood what he was reading and then used the Scriptures to explain the good news about Jesus. The Ethiopian believed and was baptized right away. This story reminds us of the power of being available and willing to share our faith when God opens doors. Philip's boldness and obedience resulted in someone coming to know Christ. For adults and teens alike, this story shows us that sharing our faith doesn't have to be forced — it can happen naturally when we listen to God's leading and step out in faith.

Key Themes:

- The importance of listening to the Holy Spirit's guidance when sharing your faith.

- How God can open doors for evangelism through natural conversations.

- The power of being ready and willing to share the gospel when opportunities arise.

Teen Devotional Recap:

- **Day 1:** *Why Sharing Your Faith is Important* – Matthew 28:19 – Jesus calls all believers to share their faith and make disciples. It's not about having all the answers, but about being willing to share the love and hope you've found in Jesus.

- **Day 2:** *How to Share Your Testimony with Others* – 1 Peter 3:15 – Your personal story of how Jesus changed your life is a powerful way to share your faith. Speak from the heart and share with gentleness and respect.

- **Day 3:** *Overcoming Fear or Nervousness About Evangelism* – 2 Timothy 1:7 – God gives us boldness through the Holy Spirit, and we don't need to be afraid to share the gospel. Trust in God's power and love to guide you.

- **Day 4:** *Building Relationships Before Sharing Your Faith* – Colossians 4:5-6 – Sharing your faith is often more effective when built on genuine relationships. Show people you care, and let your actions open the door to sharing your faith.

- **Day 5:** *Living a Life That Reflects God's Love to Others* – John 13:35 – Sometimes the best way to share your faith is through your actions. Let your kindness, humility, and joy be a testimony to God's love, making others curious to know more about Him.

Weekly Summary:

This week focused on the importance of sharing faith and practical ways to do so. Your teen learned that sharing their testimony, overcoming fear, building relationships, and living in a way that reflects God's love are all effective methods of evangelism. Evangelism is not just about words but also about actions that show people who God is. As a mentor, encourage your teen to trust God for opportunities to share their faith and to rely on the Holy Spirit for courage and guidance.

Journaling Questions for Mentor:

1. How have you experienced opportunities to share your faith? What lessons have you learned about how God uses your story to impact others?

2. Reflect on a time when you were nervous about sharing your faith. What helped you overcome that fear, and how can you encourage your teen to step out in boldness?

3. How does building relationships help open doors for sharing the gospel? How can you model this approach in your interactions with others and your teen?

4. What does it mean to live a life that reflects God's love? How can your actions be a testimony to those around you, especially your teen?

5. How can you support and encourage your teen as they share their faith with others? What steps can you take together to grow in boldness and faith?

Real-Life Story:

Nick Vujicic: Sharing Hope Without Limits

Nick Vujicic was born without arms or legs. Because of this, he faced significant challenges in his early life. Growing up, he struggled with feelings of isolation and depression, which led him to contemplate suicide as a teenager. However, during this difficult period, he found new hope and purpose through Jesus. At the age of 15, after reading a Bible verse that spoke to him about his value and purpose, he began to embrace Christianity.

He experienced a profound transformation, realizing that he could use his life to inspire others despite his physical limitations. His newfound faith motivated him to share his story, leading him to become a motivational speaker and author, and eventually, he began traveling around the world to share his story and spread the hope of Jesus. Despite his physical challenges, he uses his life as a testimony of God's love, joy, and purpose. Nick's boldness in sharing his faith inspires countless people to trust God and boldly share their faith, no matter their circumstances (Vujicic, 2010).

Discussion or Activity with Teen:

NOTE: As you go into the Activity and Conversation time this week, remember that people may argue about religion, apologetics, and doctrine, but rarely will they argue testimony, because it is your story, your personal experience.

Activity:

Go on another "treasure hunt" together, like in Week 6. In your prayer time, specifically ask God for an opportunity to share your testimonies. As you go out, look for that specific opportunity that God will provide for you to share your testimonies.

or

"Practice Your Testimony"

1. Write It Down: Encourage your teen to take a few minutes to write down their personal testimony. They can include key points like how they came to know Jesus, what He's done in their life, and how their life has changed because of their faith. Remind them that their story doesn't have to be dramatic to be meaningful — God works uniquely in everyone's life.

2. Role-Play Sharing: Practice sharing testimonies together in a relaxed, supportive way. You can start by sharing your own story first to show that everyone's journey is different and valuable.

3. Reflect on Short Sharing: Talk about how they can adapt their story for different situations, whether it's sharing with a friend or responding to a question about faith.

Debrief: After the role-play, ask the teen how they felt sharing their testimony. Did they feel nervous, excited, or encouraged? Emphasize that sharing faith is about being genuine and letting the Holy Spirit guide them in the moment.

Conversation Starter:

"Faith in Everyday Conversations"

Begin by discussing a recent conversation you had where you had the chance to mention your faith, even in a small way.

Then, ask your teen:

- "What are some situations where you feel comfortable talking about your faith, and where do you feel less comfortable?"

- "Do you think sharing your faith always has to be a big conversation, or can it be part of everyday life? Why?"

- "How do you think your actions reflect God's love and make others curious about your faith?"

Encourage your teen to start with small steps, like sharing a Bible verse that inspired them or offering to pray for a friend. This can make sharing faith feel natural and show others who God is through their daily life.

WEEK 19

UNDERSTANDING YOUR IDENTITY IN CHRIST

Introduction:

This week, your teen will explore the profound truth of their identity in Christ, learning what it means to be a child of God and how that identity influences their life. They'll consider how to reject worldly lies about self-worth and embrace their value as God's beloved. As a mentor, you can share your experiences of growing in your identity in Christ and encourage your teen to live confidently in who God made them to be.

Practical Challenge:

Teen Challenge: Take time this week to memorize a verse that reminds you of your identity in Christ. Write it down, reflect on it, and let it encourage you to live confidently in who God made you to be.

Mentor Challenge: Reflect on a verse or passage about identity that has been meaningful to you. Share it with your teen, and discuss how that truth can be a source of confidence and strength. Consider setting aside a few minutes each day to memorize the verse together, and encourage each other to live out its truth daily.

Bible Story: The Story of Gideon – Identity and Purpose (Judges 6-7)

Reflection: Gideon was a young man from the weakest clan in Israel and saw himself as the least in his family. When God called him to save Israel from the Midianites, Gideon initially doubted his own abilities and identity. Yet, God addressed him as a "mighty warrior," not because of who Gideon thought he was, but because of who God knew him to be. Despite his fears and insecurities, Gideon chose to trust in God's calling, and God used him to bring victory to Israel.

Gideon's story reminds us that our identity and purpose are rooted in who God says we are, not in how we see ourselves or what others think of us. When we embrace our identity in Christ, we can step into roles and challenges we never thought possible, trusting in God's strength rather than our own.

Key Themes:

- God sees who we truly are, even when we don't.

- Our identity is rooted in God's calling, not in our own limitations.

- Trusting God's view of us empowers us to live out our purpose with confidence.

Teen Devotional Recap:

- **Day 1:** *What It Means to Be a Child of God* – Isaiah 64:8 – Understanding that our identity is rooted in being God's beloved child, shaped by His hands and loved deeply.

- **Day 2:** *Rejecting the Lies of the World About Your Worth* – Romans 12:2 – Recognizing and rejecting the lies about our worth that come from the world, and letting God's truth renew our minds.

- **Day 3:** *Embracing Your Identity as a New Creation in Christ* – 2 Corinthians 5:17 – Understanding that in Christ, we are made new and are no longer defined by past mistakes or failures.

- **Day 4:** *How Your Identity Shapes Your Decisions and Actions* – Galatians 2:20 – Knowing who we are in Christ influences how we live, make decisions, and treat others.

- **Day 5:** *Living Confidently in Who God Says You Are* – Psalm 139:13 – Embracing the truth that we are wonderfully made by God, giving us confidence to live boldly.

Weekly Summary:

This week, your teen learned that they are deeply loved as a child of God, a new creation with purpose and value. They explored how to reject worldly lies, embrace God's truth, and live confidently in their God-given identity. The more they understand who they are in Christ, the more they can live out their faith with courage and joy.

Journaling Questions for Mentor:

1. Reflect on a time when you struggled to see yourself as God sees you. How did you overcome those doubts, and what helped you embrace your identity in Christ?

2. What worldly lies about identity and worth have you had to unlearn in your life?

3. In what ways has understanding your identity in Christ changed the way you make decisions or treat others?

4. How can you encourage others in your life to embrace their identity in Christ, especially your teen?

5. Share a time when you felt God calling you to step into something challenging. How did trusting in your identity as God's child help you face that challenge?

Real-Life Story:

Christine Caine: Living Out Your Identity in Christ

Christine Caine faced significant struggles with identity and self-worth during her early life. Growing up in Australia, she dealt with feelings of abandonment, as she was born to an unwed mother and adopted by a family that did not provide a nurturing environment. This led to deep-seated insecurities and a sense of not belonging. Throughout her youth, Christine grappled with issues of self-acceptance and often felt inadequate. However, her life began to change when she encountered the message of God's love for her.

She discovered her identity as a child of God, which became a turning point for her. Through her faith, Christine learned that her worth was not defined by her past experiences or others' opinions, but by her relationship with God. Christine's journey inspired her to share her story with others, and she became a well-known speaker and author, encouraging countless individuals to find their identity in Christ and embrace their worth as beloved children of God. Her message emphasizes the transformative power of God's love in helping us overcome struggles with identity and self-worth (Caine, 2016).

Discussion or Activity with Teen:

Activity:

Have your teen create a list of their activities, hobbies, interests, and strengths. Then have them make a list of things they think they would enjoy but are not currently involved in and areas that they wish were strengths in their lives. Next, have them put a number between 1 and 3 next to each item on the both lists. 1 represents that they feel God is most responsible for encouraging them in that area, 2 represents that they mostly encourage themselves, and 3 represents that they are mostly encouraged by others (parents, teachers, peers). Of course, there may be some overlap and they might want to put more than one number for an item and that is fine. The goal is to look back and see areas in our lives that we recognize are being encouraged by others and not by God and vice versa, to recognize areas that God may be trying to encourage us in but others may be discouraging. Sometimes, to find our identity in God, we have to first recognize and remove identities that we have taken on from others.

or

"Truth Statements"

1. Create Truth Statements: Together, brainstorm a list of "truth statements" that affirm who they are in Christ, such as:

   - "I am loved unconditionally by God."

   - "I am forgiven and made new in Christ."

   - "I am fearfully and wonderfully made."

   - "I have a unique purpose designed by God."

2. Artistic Expression: Encourage the teen to write these statements creatively — they could make a poster, design an image with digital art (it could even become their screensaver on their phone), or write each statement on index cards and decorate it to place around their room. This can serve as a daily reminder of their true identity.

3. Daily Affirmation: Challenge them to choose one or two of these truths to say to themselves each morning for the week, helping them to internalize God's view of who they are.

Debrief: Afterward, ask how it feels to declare these truths daily. Have they noticed any changes in how they see themselves or feel about challenges?

Conversation Starter:

"Replacing Lies with God's Truth"

Start by sharing an example of a common "lie" or insecurity many people face or that you have faced, like feeling unworthy or not good enough, and how God's truth counters these lies.

Then, ask your teen:

- "What's one lie you sometimes believe about yourself, and what truth from God's Word could replace it?"

- "How does knowing you're God's child and uniquely made impact how you view yourself?"

- "What steps can you take to hold onto this truth when you feel discouraged?"

Encourage your teen to remind themselves of these truths regularly, especially during moments of self-doubt, and reinforce that their value and identity are secure in Christ.

WEEK 20

OVERCOMING INSECURITY

Introduction:

This week's focus is on overcoming insecurity and embracing confidence through God's truth. Your teen will explore how to root their identity in Christ rather than seeking approval from others, replace negative thoughts with God's truth, and build self-confidence with the support of uplifting relationships. This journey will help them find security in God's unchanging love. Share your own experiences of facing insecurities and how relying on God has strengthened your confidence.

Practical Challenge:

Teen Challenge: Write down three truths about your identity in Christ from Scripture. When feelings of insecurity come up, read these truths aloud and let them remind you of your worth in God.

Mentor Challenge: Encourage your teen to choose three Bible verses that speak to their identity in Christ. Work together on memorizing these verses, and remind each other to turn to them in moments of self-doubt. Discuss specific ways to replace negative thoughts with God's truth, and check in at the end of the week to reflect on any changes in mindset.

Bible Story: Moses' Insecurity and God's Assurance (Exodus 3-4)

Reflection: Moses struggled with insecurity when God called him to lead the Israelites out of Egypt. He doubted his abilities, fearing he wasn't the right person for such a big task. Moses questioned his own worth, saying he wasn't eloquent and felt inadequate to speak on behalf of God. Yet, God assured Moses that He would be with him, giving him the strength and words he needed.

Moses' story teaches us that insecurity is common, even for those chosen by God. But rather than focusing on our own limitations, we can trust in God's power and presence. God doesn't call us based on our own strengths; He equips us for the purpose He has prepared for us. Like Moses, we can overcome insecurity by trusting that God will give us everything we need to fulfill His calling.

Key Themes:

- God sees beyond our insecurities and equips us with what we need.

- Our confidence comes from God's presence, not our own abilities.

- Trusting in God's strength helps us face challenges with boldness.

Teen Devotional Recap:

- **Day 1**: *Recognizing the Roots of Insecurity* – Psalm 139:14 – Insecurity often stems from comparison and self-doubt, but God reminds us that we are fearfully and wonderfully made.

- **Day 2**: *How to Find Security in God's Love and Approval* – Romans 8:38-39 – God's love is unchanging, and nothing can separate us from it. His love defines our worth.

- **Day 3**: *Replacing Negative Thoughts with Biblical Truth* – 2 Corinthians 10:5 – Take negative thoughts captive and replace them with God's truth about who you are.

- **Day 4**: *Building Self-Confidence in Christ* – Philippians 4:13 – Confidence grows by trusting God's strength rather than our own abilities.

- **Day 5**: *Surrounding Yourself with Uplifting People* – Proverbs 27:17 – Uplifting friendships encourage us to embrace our identity in Christ and grow confidently.

Weekly Summary:

This week, your teen learned to overcome insecurity by focusing on God's truth about their worth, finding security in His love, replacing negative thoughts with biblical truth, building self-confidence in Christ, and surrounding themselves with uplifting friends. By rooting their identity in God, they can confidently face challenges, knowing that their worth is secure in Him.

Journaling Questions for Mentor:

1. Reflect on a time when you struggled with insecurity. What helped you find confidence in God rather than seeking approval from others?

2. What verses or truths from Scripture remind you of your worth and identity in Christ?

3. When you face self-doubt, how do you remind yourself of God's unchanging love?

4. How have positive friendships encouraged your confidence and faith?

5. In what areas of life do you still struggle with insecurity, and how can you lean on God to overcome it?

Real-Life Story:

Lecrae: Finding Confidence in God's Truth

Lecrae, now a famous Christian hip-hop and rap artist, faced significant struggles with identity and self-worth throughout his life, particularly during his formative years. Growing up in a challenging environment marked by instability, he dealt with issues like poverty and the absence of a father figure. These experiences contributed to feelings of confusion about his identity and low self-esteem. As a teenager, Lecrae turned to various outlets, including music and hip-hop culture, seeking validation and a sense of belonging. However, he often found himself in destructive behaviors and a lifestyle that didn't align with his values, leading to deeper feelings of emptiness.

His transformative journey began when he encountered Christ in college. Through his faith, Lecrae discovered a new perspective on his identity. He learned that his worth wasn't tied to his past, his accomplishments, or the opinions of others, but rather rooted in being a child of God. This realization helped him embrace his true identity and value. Lecrae's faith journey fueled his passion for creating music that reflects his beliefs and experiences. He began to share his story through his lyrics, addressing themes of hope, redemption, and self-acceptance. As he grew in his faith, Lecrae gained confidence, recognizing that he was loved and chosen by God. His journey serves as a testament to the power of faith in transforming lives and reshaping identities (Lecrae, 2020).

Discussion or Activity with Teen:

Activity:

Help the teen identify one practical step they can take in overcoming a specific insecurity they have and then coach and encourage them in that step. It might be inviting a friend or acquaintance into this journey of discovery with God, confronting a hard issue in their lives that requires a difficult conversation with someone, trying out for a sports team, or signing up for an overseas mission trip to get them out of their comfort zone. Discover God's empowering grace together through the journey.

or

"Truth Journal"

1. Identify Insecurities: Invite the teen to privately jot down a few insecurities or negative thoughts they experience (e.g., "I'm not good enough," "I don't fit in," "I'm not as talented as others").

2. Replace with Truth: For each insecurity, have them look up a Bible verse that speaks to their worth and identity in Christ. Some helpful verses include Psalm 139:14, 1 Peter 2:9, and Ephesians 2:10. Encourage them to write these verses alongside each negative thought, replacing lies with biblical truth.

3. Create Daily Affirmations: Help them turn these truths into daily affirmations, like "I am God's masterpiece," "I am chosen and loved," and "I have unique gifts and a purpose." Encourage them to review these affirmations each morning to start their day with God's perspective.

Debrief: After a few days, check in with them about how focusing on these truths has affected their mindset.

Conversation Starter:

"Building Confidence in God's Truth"

Share any story you have about overcoming insecurity and then begin with a general question about self-confidence and discuss why it can be easy to feel insecure. Then, shift the conversation to how understanding God's love can transform these feelings.

Ask questions such as:

- "When you feel insecure, what helps you remember your value in God's eyes?"

- "How can focusing on God's truth about who you are make a difference when you're feeling down?"

- "Who are people in your life who encourage you and remind you of your worth in Christ?"

Encourage them to hold onto these truths and people as a support system, especially in challenging times. Remind them that real confidence comes from knowing they are fully loved by God, no matter what.

WEEK 21

DEALING WITH FEAR AND ANXIETY

Introduction:

This week, the focus is on helping your teen learn to manage fear and anxiety by turning to God's promises and practicing healthy ways of coping. They will be encouraged to understand that, while fear is a part of life, God's presence and peace can bring comfort in every situation. Consider sharing your own experiences of fear and how you have relied on faith to find peace, and be open to listening as they express their own worries or concerns.

Practical Challenge:

Teen Challenge: Find a verse that brings you peace and write it down somewhere where you can see it daily. Whenever fear or anxiety arises, read that verse and let it remind you of God's presence, peace, and power over every situation.

Mentor Challenge: Encourage your teen to find a verse about peace that resonates with them and write it down somewhere visible, like their room, notebook, or even on their phone background. Suggest they make it a habit to read the verse whenever they feel anxious or afraid. You might even choose a verse together to memorize or discuss, focusing on how it can remind you both of God's promises.

Bible Story: Jesus Calms the Storm (Mark 4:35-41)

Reflection: One evening, Jesus and His disciples were in a boat crossing the Sea of Galilee. As they traveled, a fierce storm arose, and waves began crashing into the boat. The disciples were terrified and believed they would drown. But Jesus was calmly sleeping in the stern of the boat. In their fear, the disciples woke Him up, crying out for help. Jesus arose, rebuked the wind, and said to the sea, "Peace, be still!" Immediately, the storm ceased, and there was a great calm.

Jesus then asked His disciples, "Why are you so afraid? Do you still have no faith?" This story teaches us that Jesus is present and in control, even in life's storms. When fear and anxiety overwhelm us, we can call on Jesus, who has power over every situation. Trusting in His presence brings peace, even when circumstances feel uncertain.

Key Themes:

- Jesus is with us in every storm, ready to bring peace.

- When fear arises, we can trust Jesus' power over our circumstances.

- Jesus' peace calms us and brings courage, even when life feels out of control.

Teen Devotional Recap:

- **Day 1:** *Understanding That Fear Is a Part of Life* – John 16:33 – Fear is part of living in a fallen world, but Jesus has overcome it, and His presence brings peace.

- **Day 2:** *Trusting God in the Midst of Your Fears* – Psalm 56:3-4 – Trust in God's strength when fear arises; He is greater than any challenge.

- **Day 3:** *Praying for Peace in Anxious Times* – Philippians 4:6-7 – Bring every worry to God in prayer, allowing His peace to guard your heart and mind.

- **Day 4:** *Meditating on Scriptures That Calm Fear and Anxiety* – Isaiah 41:10 – Use Scripture to anchor your heart in God's promises.

- **Day 5:** *Developing Healthy Coping Mechanisms with God's Help* – Romans 8:15 – With God's help, create habits that help you handle anxiety in a positive way.

Weekly Summary:

This week, your teen learned about managing fear and anxiety through trust in God, prayer, meditating on Scripture, and healthy coping mechanisms, such as journaling, exercising, and seeking good community. Fear may be unavoidable, but they can return to peace in God's presence and rely on His power in every situation.

Journaling Questions for Mentor:

1. Reflect on a time when you faced fear or anxiety. How did prayer or Scripture help you find peace?

2. What are some Bible verses that bring you comfort and remind you of God's presence during anxious times?

3. How can you encourage your teen to bring their fears to God and rely on His peace?

4. What healthy coping mechanisms have helped you manage anxiety, and how can you share these with your teen?

5. Is there a current fear or worry in your life that you can ask God for peace in?

Real-Life Story:

Max Lucado: Battling Fear with God's Truth

Max Lucado, a Christian author and pastor, struggled with anxiety throughout his life. In his book *Anxious for Nothing*, Lucado has openly shared his struggles with anxiety, particularly during a challenging period in his life when he faced immense pressure as a pastor and author. He experienced feelings of being overwhelmed, leading to sleepless nights and a persistent sense of worry. This battle with anxiety caused him to question his abilities and left him feeling inadequate. In the midst of this struggle, Lucado turned to the Lord for strength and comfort. He found solace in Scripture, particularly verses that emphasize God's presence and reassurance. He began to meditate on passages that spoke of God's peace, such as Philippians 4:6-7, which encourages believers not to be anxious but to bring their concerns to God in prayer.

Through prayer and reflection, Lucado learned to replace his anxious thoughts with reminders of God's faithfulness. He developed practical strategies to cope with his anxiety, including journaling and deepening his prayer life. This process helped him to shift his focus from his fears to God's promises. Lucado writes, "The presence of anxiety is unavoidable, but the prison of anxiety is optional."

His story teaches that while fear and anxiety may be part of life, God's truth has the power to set you free and fill you with peace (Lucado, 2017).

Discussion or Activity with Teen:

Activity:

Together, read Mark 4:35-41, the story of Jesus calming the storm. Discuss the disciples' fear and how Jesus responded. Ask the teen if there are "storms" in their life that feel overwhelming, and talk about how trusting Jesus can bring peace, even if circumstances haven't changed. Encourage them to pray whenever they feel fearful, asking Jesus to bring calm to their hearts. For fun, pick an activity that might seem a little challenging and do it together, whether it be ice skating, rock climbing in a gym, or bungee jumping, and have a fun practical victory over fear that will also help you bond with your teen. You might have to get out of your comfort zone to encourage your teen to get out of theirs.

or

"Casting Cares Prayer Box"

1. Create a "Cares Box": Provide the teen with a small box or container, which they can decorate if they wish. Explain that this will be a place for them to "cast their cares" on God (1 Peter 5:7).

2. Write Down Worries: Encourage them to write down any fears or anxieties they're dealing with on small slips of paper and place them in the box, symbolizing giving their worries over to God.

3. Pray and Release: Guide them to pray over each worry before placing it in the box, asking God to take control and bring them peace.

4. Review and Reflect: After a week, revisit the box with them and talk about any changes in their anxiety levels. Did praying and letting go help them feel more at peace? Did they notice God's presence more as they trusted Him?

Debrief: This activity can help them visualize releasing their fears to God, knowing that He's in control. If the activity seems helpful, it is something that could be continued for as long as needed. When certain fears are completely gone, remove them from the box, throw them away, or even burn them to symbolize the victory that God has given over that fear.

Conversation Starter:

"Finding Peace in God's Presence"

Share one of your personal stories about dealing with fear and then start by asking your teen what they experience when they're feeling anxious or afraid. Transition to a discussion about where they've seen God's peace at work in their lives, even in difficult situations.

Ask questions like:

- "What's one thing that helps you feel calmer when you're worried?"

- "How do you think praying or meditating on Scripture can help with anxiety?"

- "When was a time you felt God's presence in a situation where you were nervous or afraid?"

Encourage them to share any Bible verses that comfort them. Reassure them that God cares about their fears and that leaning on Him can bring peace even in the most challenging times.

WEEK 22

HANDLING STRESS

Introduction:

This week centers on teaching your teen healthy ways to manage stress by bringing their concerns to God, creating routines for rest, and learning practical tips for handling pressures. You might discuss your own experiences with managing stress and share how relying on God has helped you through challenging times. Let them know they are not alone in feeling overwhelmed and that God provides both peace and practical wisdom to navigate stressful seasons.

Practical Challenge:

Teen Challenge: Create a daily routine that includes rest and time with God. Set aside time each day to pray, read the Bible, and rest in God's presence. Let this routine help you handle stress and experience God's peace.

Mentor Challenge: Encourage your teen to create a daily routine that includes rest and time with God. Suggest they choose one or two stress-relieving activities (e.g. taking a walk in nature or listening to instrumental praise music) and commit to spending time in prayer or reading Scripture each day. This can help build a habit of finding peace and balance amid the busyness of life. If you don't already have a routine of rest with God, join your teen in this challenge.

Bible Story: Mary and Martha (Luke 10:38-42)

Reflection: Mary and Martha were two sisters who welcomed Jesus into their home. While Martha was busy with all the preparations, Mary chose to sit at Jesus' feet and listen to His teaching. Martha became frustrated, asking Jesus to tell Mary to help her with the work. But Jesus responded by saying, "Martha, Martha, you are worried and upset about many things, but few things are needed—or indeed only one. Mary has chosen what is better, and it will not be taken away from her."

This story teaches us that while responsibilities are important, spending time with God is essential for our peace and well-being. When we're stressed and overwhelmed, choosing to be like Mary—taking time to sit with Jesus—helps us refocus and find rest in His presence.

Key Themes:

- Prioritizing time with God can bring peace in the midst of busyness.

- It's okay to pause from responsibilities to spend time with Jesus.

- Seeking Jesus first helps us manage our stress more effectively.

Teen Devotional Recap:

- **Day 1:** *Identifying the Main Sources of Stress in Your Life* – Matthew 11:28-29 – Jesus invites us to bring our burdens to Him and find rest.

- **Day 2:** *The Importance of Rest and Time with God* – Isaiah 30:15 – True strength comes from being still and spending time with God.

- **Day 3:** *How to Manage Your Time Effectively to Reduce Stress* – Ephesians 5:15-16 – Using time wisely and setting priorities helps reduce stress.

- **Day 4:** *Practical Tips for Handling School, Sports, and Other Pressures* – Isaiah 40:31 – Trusting God's strength helps us handle the pressures of life.

- **Day 5:** *Trusting God with Your Worries* – 1 Peter 5:7 – We can cast all our worries on God, knowing He cares for us.

Weekly Summary:

This week, your teen explored ways to handle stress by identifying its sources, finding rest in God, managing their time, and trusting God with their worries. They learned that Jesus invites us to find peace and renewal in Him and that prioritizing time with God is essential for managing stress.

Journaling Questions for Mentor:

1. What are some ways that stress impacts your life? How do you handle it when things feel overwhelming?

2. How do you prioritize rest and time with God, even during busy or stressful seasons?

3. What practical steps help you manage your time effectively and set priorities?

4. How does trusting God help you handle stress, and how can you share this perspective with your teen?

5. Reflect on a time when leaning on God's presence brought you peace during a stressful situation.

Real-Life Story:

Tim Tebow: Handling Stress Through Faith

Tim Tebow, former NFL quarterback and current sports commentator, faced immense pressure on and off the field throughout his career. However, Tebow consistently emphasized that his identity is rooted in his faith in God rather than in his performance on the field. This mindset helped him avoid feeling overwhelmed by the constant scrutiny of his career, whether as a Heisman Trophy-winning college quarterback, an NFL player, or a professional baseball player. In the face of criticism, stress, and high expectations, Tebow leaned on his faith. He once said, "No matter how much stress or pressure you're under, know that God is always with you" (Tebow, 2016). This perspective helped shield him from the emotional highs and lows associated with public opinion. Tim's example shows that, by placing your trust in God, you can handle life's pressures with confidence, peace, and perseverance.

Discussion or Activity with Teen:

Activity:

Together, read Luke 10:38-42 about Mary and Martha. Discuss how Martha's busyness left her feeling stressed and how Mary's choice to spend time with Jesus brought peace. Ask your teen if they relate more to Martha or Mary in this season of life. Encourage them to create a "quiet time" routine with God, even if it's just five minutes a day apart from this devotional, and talk about how this can help bring calm during busy times. Along with quiet times, encourage your teen to also find other practical ways to rest, such as inviting your teen for a hike in nature or to a symphony. Help them discover activities that promote true rest and renewal. Make sure they understand the difference between avoidance/distraction and true rest. Otherwise many teens will be tempted to think time on their device, social media, video game playing, and movies are a time of rest. They need you, as a mentor, to not just tell them the difference, but do everything in your power to help them experience the difference. Many of us as adults also need this reminder for ourselves.

or

"Creating a Rest & Recharge Plan"

1. Identify Stressors: Start by helping your teen list some of the main sources of stress in their life, whether it's school, relationships, activities, or personal challenges.

2. Build a "Rest & Recharge" Plan: Encourage them to create a simple plan for moments when they're feeling stressed. Have them choose activities they find restful (e.g., praying, reading Scripture, taking a short walk, listening to worship music). They can specifically plan these "rest" times before or after things in their schedule that they know cause stress.

3. Incorporate Time with God: Help them identify specific times in their day or week to spend with God in prayer, Scripture, or reflection. Emphasize that even a few minutes can make a difference in managing stress.

4. Create Reminders: Suggest writing reminders or setting alarms to prompt them to take a break and reset when feeling overwhelmed. They could write down a favorite verse about peace or rest (e.g., Matthew 11:28) and place it somewhere visible.

Debrief: Talk about how having a plan can make it easier to handle stress when it arises, reminding them that God is always with them and ready to provide peace.

Conversation Starter:

"What Does Resting in God Look Like?"

Share your story about learning to rest and begin by asking your teen about times when they feel the most relaxed and renewed. Discuss how spending time with God can provide a unique kind of rest that goes beyond physical relaxation. As discussed above, make sure they understand the difference between avoidance/distraction and true rest.

Ask questions like:

- "What activities or practices make you feel more at peace when you're stressed?"

- "How do you feel after spending time with God, whether through prayer, worship, or simply sitting in silence?"

- "What are some ways we can remind ourselves to pause and reconnect with God when things feel overwhelming?"

Encourage them to share any verses or habits they find helpful for handling stress. Emphasize that God cares about their well-being and invites them to find true rest in Him.

WEEK 23

DEVELOPING SELF-DISCIPLINE

Introduction:

This week's theme focuses on building self-discipline in various aspects of life, especially in spiritual growth. Encourage your teen by sharing your own experiences of how setting goals, developing good habits, and relying on God's strength has helped you grow in self-discipline. Let them know that discipline is a journey, one that God is actively part of, helping us each step of the way.

Practical Challenge:

Teen Challenge: Set one spiritual goal for yourself this week and create a plan to stick to it. Whether it's a daily prayer time, Bible reading plan, serving others, or continuing the challenge from last week, commit to your goal and ask God for the discipline to see it through.

Mentor Challenge: Encourage your teen to set a small, achievable spiritual goal for the week, such as reading a chapter of the Bible daily or spending five minutes in prayer each morning. Help them plan how they can incorporate this goal into their routine and check in with them on their progress. Let them know that discipline is a journey, and it's okay to start small and build from there.

Bible Story: Daniel's Consistent Discipline (Daniel 6:1-10)

Reflection: Daniel was a man of discipline, and his daily habits of prayer and worship helped him stay connected to God, even in challenging circumstances. When King Darius issued a decree that everyone should pray only to him, Daniel continued his usual practice of praying to God three times a day. Daniel's commitment to his routine and his willingness to honor God above all else shows the power of self-discipline.

Key Themes:

- Consistency in spiritual habits can strengthen your faith and courage.

- Self-discipline helps you remain faithful, even under pressure.

- Trusting God gives you the strength to prioritize Him over any earthly demands.

Teen Devotional Recap:

- **Day 1:** *Why Self-Discipline Is Important for Spiritual Growth* – 1 Corinthians 9:24-25 – Discipline leads to spiritual growth and a deeper relationship with God.

- **Day 2:** *Setting Goals and Sticking to Them* – Proverbs 21:5 – Setting goals helps us stay focused and motivated.

- **Day 3:** *Overcoming Laziness and Procrastination* – Proverbs 13:4 – Hard work and diligence lead to growth and fulfillment.

- **Day 4:** *Learning to Say "No" to Distractions* – 2 Timothy 2:4-7 – Staying focused on God's purpose requires saying no to distractions.

- **Day 5:** *How to Grow in Self-Discipline with God's Help* – Philippians 2:13 – God provides the desire and strength to pursue what pleases Him.

Weekly Summary:

This week, your teen learned about developing self-discipline as an essential part of spiritual growth. Setting goals, overcoming procrastination, avoiding distractions, and relying on God's help are key elements in building self-discipline. Growing in self-discipline leads to a closer walk with God and a life more aligned with His purpose.

Journaling Questions for Mentor:

1. How has self-discipline impacted your relationship with God? In what areas has it helped you grow?

2. What are some spiritual or personal goals that you are working on, and what

steps help you stay consistent?

3. How do you handle distractions or laziness in your spiritual life, and what strategies have you found helpful?

4. Where do you see God actively helping you grow in self-discipline, even when it's challenging?

5. Reflect on a time when practicing self-discipline helped you overcome a specific challenge or temptation.

Real-Life Story:

Hudson Taylor: A Life of Spiritual Discipline

Hudson Taylor, a missionary to China and the founder of the China Inland Mission, was known not only for his pioneering work in missions but also for his deep spiritual disciplines. Taylor practiced consistent daily habits of prayer, Bible reading, and fasting, which gave him strength to face the challenges of his ministry. He once said, "Do not have your concert first and tune your instruments afterward. Begin the day with God" (Taylor, 1997). His life demonstrated that spiritual disciplines are not burdens but pathways to deeper intimacy with God and greater strength for His work. Taylor's story encourages us to make spiritual disciplines a priority and to seek God first in everything we do.

Discussion or Activity with Teen:

Activity:

Discuss the importance of setting consistent habits. Ask your teen to set a goal for growing spiritually, emotionally, mentally, and physically, one goal for each category. They will need your help to set these goals (for example, memorize one verse a week for one month, end an unhealthy relationship by the end of the month, set aside 2 hours/weekday to study and do homework for one month, and run 15 minutes/day for at least 20 days this month). Encourage them to start with small, achievable goals and remind them that discipline is a journey, and God's strength is with them every step of the way. Encourage the setting of SMART (Specific, Measurable, Achievable, Relevant, and Time-bound) goals. Then put the dates in your calendars for each goal and maybe a reminder at the halfway point to check in. On the due dates review the progress that was made. There is no shame in not completing a task, but encourage them to set a new date and keep moving forward. For the tasks that have been completed, consider a new goal to replace it. The goal is to be in the process of changing their habits with God's help. If you want to go the extra mile, set your own goals and have a friendly competition in achieving the goals.

or

"Setting a Self-Discipline Challenge"

1. Identify an Area for Growth: Help your teen choose one area where they'd like to grow in self-discipline, whether it's spending more time in prayer, reading Scripture daily, limiting social media, or completing tasks on time.

2. Set a Clear Goal: Work together to set a realistic, achievable goal. For example, if they want to read the Bible daily, they could set a goal to read a few verses each morning or evening for the next week.

3. Track Progress: Encourage them to create a simple tracking system (e.g., a checklist, notes on their phone, or a journal) where they can mark their progress each day. The goal is to celebrate small wins and stay motivated.

4. Reflect and Adjust: At the end of the week, have them review how the challenge went, noting what helped them stay disciplined and what obstacles they encountered. Discuss any adjustments they'd like to make for future growth.

Debrief: Talk about how self-discipline is a journey and how each step forward, even small ones, builds stronger habits and a closer relationship with God.

Conversation Starter:

"How Can Self-Discipline Draw Us Closer to God?"

Share where you are at in your own journey towards self-discipline and start by asking your teen to consider how self-discipline in one area can impact other parts of their life. Discuss how setting goals and practicing discipline, even in simple ways, can help them feel more aligned with God's purpose.

Ask questions like:

- "What's one area where you feel you'd like to grow in self-discipline?"

- "How do you think working on self-discipline could help you feel closer to God?"

- "Are there any distractions or habits that make it hard to stay focused on what matters most?"

Encourage them to think of self-discipline as a way to honor God and prepare their heart to hear from Him more clearly. Let them know that God is there to help them with each step in their growth.

WEEK 24

NAVIGATING SOCIAL MEDIA AND SELF-WORTH

Introduction:

This week's theme focuses on helping your teen develop a healthy relationship with social media and find their identity in Christ rather than in online feedback. As social media continues to be a significant part of teens' lives, it's important to guide them in recognizing its impact on self-worth and learning to use it positively. Share your experiences with navigating online spaces, focusing on what has helped you stay rooted in God's perspective rather than others' opinions.

Practical Challenge:

Teen Challenge: Choose one way to use your social media to spread encouragement and positivity this week. It could be sharing an uplifting Bible verse, sending a kind message to a friend, or posting something that reflects God's love and truth.

Mentor Challenge: Encourage your teen to think about how they can use their social media positively this week. Suggest simple acts, like sharing a verse, posting a gratitude list, or complimenting someone genuinely. Do the same on your social media to help set the example. Remind them that small acts of encouragement can have a big impact, especially when done with a heart for God.

Bible Story: Jesus' Identity in Temptation (Matthew 4:1-11)

Reflection: In this story, Jesus faces temptation in the wilderness, where Satan tries to challenge His identity as the Son of God. Each temptation pushes Jesus to prove Himself, but Jesus stands firm, rooted in God's truth, without needing validation or approval from others. He models the strength that comes from knowing who we are in God, showing that we don't need to prove ourselves by the world's standards.

Key Themes:

- Identity in God: Jesus didn't need to prove who He was to others. His identity was secure in His relationship with God.

- Confidence in God's Word: Jesus relied on Scripture to counter the lies and pressure from Satan.

- Resilience Against Temptation: Jesus resisted the need for external validation, showing us that we don't need others' approval when we know God's truth.

Teen Devotional Recap:

- **Day 1:** *How Social Media Can Influence Your Self-Image* – 2 Corinthians 10:12,17-18 – God's approval is what truly matters, not how we appear online.

- **Day 2:** *Finding Your Worth in God, Not in Likes or Followers* – Zephaniah 3:17 – Your worth is found in God's love, not in social media metrics.

- **Day 3:** *Setting Healthy Boundaries with Social Media Use* – 1 Corinthians 6:12 – Set boundaries to prevent social media from impacting your mental health.

- **Day 4:** *Avoiding Comparison with Others Online* – Isaiah 25:1 – Avoid comparing yourself to others by focusing on God's purpose for you.

- **Day 5:** *Using Social Media to Positively Impact Others* – Psalm 71:15-16 – Use social media to share God's love and be a positive influence.

Weekly Summary:

This week's study highlighted the importance of navigating social media with a focus on self-worth in Christ. Teens learned to set boundaries, avoid comparison, and use their online presence positively, all while remembering that their worth is rooted in God's love, not in likes or followers. By relying on God's truth, they can use social media in a way that honors God and encourages others.

Journaling Questions for Mentor:

1. How does social media impact the way you see yourself? Are there any specific ways it influences your thoughts or actions?

2. How can setting boundaries help you maintain a healthy relationship with social media and stay focused on what truly matters?

3. When do you find yourself tempted to seek validation from others, and how do you remind yourself of your worth in God during those times?

4. In what ways can you use your social media presence to encourage, uplift, and reflect God's love to others?

5. What are some truths from Scripture that you can meditate on when you feel the pull to compare yourself to others online?

Real-Life Story:

Sadie Robertson Huff: Using Social Media for God's Glory

Sadie Robertson Huff, a Christian author, speaker, and social media influencer, who largely gained influence through her appearance on the reality TV show *Duck Dynasty,* is known for using her online platform to spread faith, positivity, and encouragement. She's faced pressure from social media but learned to find her worth in God instead of likes or followers. Sadie says, "Don't let social media be the place you find your worth; let it be the place you show others where they can find theirs" (Huff, 2020). Her life shows that when you use social media with purpose, it can be a powerful tool to glorify God and uplift others.

Discussion or Activity with Teen:

Activity:

Take time with your teen to create a "Social Media Purpose Statement" that reflects how they want to represent themselves and their faith online. Ask questions like, "What message do you want to share with others? How do you want people to feel when they see your posts?" Encourage them to keep this statement somewhere visible as a reminder of their God-centered purpose on social media.

or

"Social Media Self-Reflection Challenge"

1. Evaluate Current Habits: Ask your teen to take a few moments to assess how they currently use social media. This can include the amount of time spent on different platforms, the types of content they consume, and how social media typically makes them feel. **NOTE:** Check the app usage settings on the phone, as most of us do not realize how much time we actually spend on social media. If those settings have been turned off, turn them on and re-evaluate after one week.

2. Set a Social Media Goal: Together, set one or two intentional goals for using social media positively and with purpose. This could involve limiting screen time, unfollowing accounts that lead to comparison, or sharing content that uplifts others.

3. Track and Reflect: Encourage your teen to keep a short log of how they feel after using social media each day. Did they feel inspired, grateful, or encouraged? Or did they feel stressed, anxious, or envious? Have them note any positive changes from following their new goals.

4. Review and Pray: At the end of the week, review their experiences together. Discuss what they learned and pray for guidance to continue using social media in a way that brings peace, positivity, and reflects their worth in Christ.

Debrief: Talk about how even small changes can make social media a healthier experience and align with God's vision for their life.

Conversation Starter:

"How Does Social Media Affect Your Self-Worth?"

Share your own battle with social media and begin by discussing how social media can sometimes create pressure to look or act a certain way. Ask questions to encourage reflection, such as:

- "Do you feel more positive or negative after spending time on social media?" **NOTE:** It is important to recognize the difference between the immediate release of endorphins created by social engineers while you're on your device (watch "The Social Dilemma" on Netflix for more on this) and the discontentment that comes after those endorphins go away.

- "How can remembering your worth in Christ help you navigate social media with more peace?"

- "What are some ways you think God could use social media to impact others positively?"

Help your teen explore how keeping their self-worth rooted in God's love can transform their experience on social media, allowing them to see it as a tool for good rather than a source of comparison.

WEEK 25

EMBRACING GOD'S PURPOSE FOR YOUR LIFE

Introduction:

This week's focus is on helping teens understand that God has a unique purpose for each of us. Finding and embracing this purpose can take time, patience, and trust in God's plan. By reflecting on their gifts, seeking God's will, and taking faithful steps, they can begin to see God's purpose unfold in their lives. Share your personal experiences of discerning God's purpose, whether it was through prayer, patience, or unexpected opportunities.

Practical Challenge:

Teen Challenge: Pray this week for God to reveal His purpose for your life. Ask Him to show you how to use your gifts to serve others and to guide you step by step in His perfect plan. Look for small opportunities to act on God's purpose each day.

Mentor Challenge: Encourage the teen to pray specifically for God to reveal His purpose for them this week. Suggest they keep a notebook or journal nearby to write down any thoughts, ideas, or moments where they feel God's guidance. Let them know that sometimes God's purpose is revealed in small actions, such as helping others, showing kindness, or serving in their community. Be sure to share with them any gifts and talents that you see in them to encourage them.

Bible Story: Joseph's Journey from Dreams to Destiny (Genesis 37, 39-50)

Reflection: Joseph's story shows how God can work through every season of our lives, even the painful ones, to bring about His purpose. From being sold into slavery by his brothers to being falsely accused and imprisoned, Joseph endured many hardships. Yet he trusted God and remained faithful. Eventually, he rose to a position of great power in Egypt, where he saved many lives during a famine — including the lives of his own family. Joseph's journey teaches us that God's purpose is not always revealed immediately, and sometimes it takes years to understand how God was working all along.

Key Themes:

- Trusting God's Plan Amid Hardship: Even in suffering, Joseph trusted God's purpose for his life.

- Faithfulness in Every Situation: Despite being mistreated, Joseph remained faithful, serving God wherever he was placed.

- God's Timing and Redemption: God used Joseph's story for a greater purpose, redeeming difficult circumstances to save many people.

Teen Devotional Recap:

- **Day 1:** *Discovering Your God-Given Talents and Abilities* – 1 Peter 4:10 – God gifts each of us uniquely; our talents are meant to serve others and glorify Him.

- **Day 2:** *How to Seek God's Will for Your Life* – Matthew 6:33 – By seeking God first, we align ourselves with His purpose.

- **Day 3:** *Being Patient in Finding Your Purpose* – Psalm 37:7 – Patience is essential as we trust God's timing in revealing our purpose.

- **Day 4:** *Trusting God Even When His Plan is Unclear* – Psalm 138:8 – Even when we don't understand, God's plans for us are always good.

- **Day 5:** *Taking Small Steps Toward Fulfilling Your Purpose* – Colossians 3:23 – Purpose unfolds as we work faithfully in each moment, doing all for God's glory.

Weekly Summary:

This week, teens learned that God has a specific purpose for each of them. By discovering their gifts, seeking God's guidance, practicing patience, and trusting His plan, they can take faithful steps toward fulfilling their purpose. God's purpose is rarely revealed all at once; it's a journey of daily obedience and trust in His perfect timing.

Journaling Questions for Mentor:

1. How has your understanding of God's purpose for your life evolved over the years? What has helped you discern His calling?

2. In what ways have patience and trust played a role in following God's plan?

3. What small steps are you currently taking toward fulfilling God's purpose, and how do they reflect your desire to serve Him?

4. How do you recognize and use your God-given gifts in daily life? Are there additional talents you feel God is calling you to develop?

5. Reflecting on Lottie Moon's story, how can you commit to serving God's purpose in a way that makes a lasting impact?

Real-Life Story:

Lottie Moon: Embracing God's Purpose in Missions

Lottie Moon was a missionary to China who dedicated her life to sharing the gospel with the Chinese people. Lottie Moon's call to serve in China came during a transformative period in her life. As a young woman, she was well-educated and initially skeptical of Christianity, even mocking religious gatherings. However, during a revival meeting at her college, she experienced a profound change of heart and committed her life to Christ. This decision sparked a desire to serve God in a deeper way.

In 1873, while working as a teacher, Lottie began to feel a strong burden for missions, especially for those who had never heard the gospel. She became captivated by stories of China's vast, unreached population and realized that few missionaries were ministering to Chinese women, who had little chance to hear the gospel. Despite her family's doubts and society's limited acceptance of women missionaries, she felt an undeniable call to go.

Lottie finally answered God's call and traveled to China, where she devoted over 40 years of her life to sharing the gospel, teaching, and advocating for missions. Her commitment and sacrifices, including giving away her own food during times of famine, left a legacy that continues to inspire missionary work today. Despite facing loneliness, hardship, and illness, she embraced God's purpose with faith and determination. Lottie once said, "I have a firm conviction that I am immortal till my work is done" (Cannon, 1997). Her passion to serve others and fulfill God's calling on her life left a lasting impact on missions around the world. Lottie's story reminds us that when we embrace God's purpose, we can make a difference that lasts beyond our lifetime.

Discussion or Activity with Teen:

Activity:

Discover one of the teen's "hidden" talents, a talent that is recognized by them, you, or someone else that the teen is not using at all. Create an opportunity for them to use that talent. If they can cook, set up a dinner party that they cook for. If they are compassionate, take them to a soup kitchen or other social ministry where they can serve. If they are a leader or teacher, encourage them to take on or help in a Sunday School classroom for younger children. Be creative and encouraging, but not pushy.

or

"Exploring Your Gifts and Talents"

1. Identify Gifts: Ask the teen to write down their strengths, talents, and interests. This can include academic strengths, creative skills, hobbies, or character traits (like being a good listener or problem-solver).

2. Seek Feedback: Encourage the teen to ask a trusted friend, family member, or mentor what strengths they see in them. This can help them recognize gifts they may overlook or take for granted.

3. Reflect on How to Use These Gifts for God: Together, discuss how these strengths and talents could be used in ways that honor God and serve others. They could consider using their creativity for community projects, their compassion to encourage others, or their leadership skills in church activities.

4. Create a "Purpose Prayer": Guide the teen in creating a short prayer asking God for direction on using their gifts and talents to fulfill His purpose for them. They can keep this prayer and revisit it often as they grow and explore their calling.

Debrief: Talk about how discovering purpose is a journey and that each strength and interest God has given can play a role in His larger plan.

Conversation Starter:

"What Do You Think God Created You To Do?"

Start by discussing the teen's unique interests and strengths, asking questions such as:

- "What activities or subjects bring you the most joy and energy?"

- "Have you ever felt that God was leading you in a particular direction?"

- "How could these gifts be used to make a positive impact on others?"

NOTE: It is important the teen does not feel pushed to decide "what they want to do with their life", but instead that they feel encouraged to explore the talents God has given them.

This conversation can open their heart to see their talents as part of God's purpose, helping them realize that their gifts aren't accidental but intentionally placed by God to serve His kingdom.

WEEK 26

BALANCING SCHOOL, FRIENDS, AND FAITH

Introduction:

This week's focus is on helping teens navigate the busyness of school, friendships, and their faith commitments. Maintaining a balanced life can be challenging, especially when so many activities compete for their attention. As you guide your teen, share your own experiences with time management, setting priorities, and finding balance. Encourage them to see God's guidance as essential in creating balance that honors Him.

Practical Challenge:

Teen Challenge: Choose one area of your life where you need to manage your time better and set a goal for improvement this week. Ask God for wisdom in prioritizing your time, and commit to making changes that help you grow closer to Him and balance your life well.

Mentor Challenge: Just as the teen's challenge encourages them to prioritize, consider one area where you could use better balance this week. Set a small, achievable goal to help manage this area with God's guidance — perhaps an intentional quiet time, a set break from technology, or dedicating time to prayer. Help keep each other accountable to reach your goals.

Bible Story: Jesus' Balance of Ministry and Rest (Mark 6:30-32)

Reflection: In Mark 6, after the disciples had been actively teaching and serving, Jesus recognized their need for rest. He invited them to "come away" to a quiet place, away from the crowds and responsibilities. This shows us that even in ministry, Jesus valued rest and balance. Jesus modeled that while serving and engaging with others is important, taking time to recharge and be with God is also essential.

Key Themes:

- Rest and Recharge: Jesus invites us to step back and rest, even when we feel there is more to do.

- Setting Priorities: Jesus balanced His ministry work with moments of quiet and prayer, showing that time with God is crucial.

- Trusting in God's Timing: There is a season for all things. Jesus modeled trusting God to make the most of every moment.

Teen Devotional Recap:

- **Day 1:** *Setting Priorities to Keep God First* – Matthew 22:37-38 – Loving God wholeheartedly is the foundation of life; putting Him first helps align all other priorities.

- **Day 2:** *How to Manage Your Time Effectively* – Colossians 4:5 – Making the most of every opportunity by managing time well honors God and reduces stress.

- **Day 3:** *Making Sure Faith is a Priority in a Busy Schedule* – Psalm 119:105 – Even brief daily time with God's Word lights the path, offering guidance and peace.

- **Day 4:** *Finding Balance Between School, Friends, and Activities* – Ecclesiastes 3:1 – Balance comes from understanding each season's purpose and trusting God's timing.

- **Day 5:** *Relying on God's Strength When Life Feels Overwhelming* – Isaiah 40:29 – God renews strength when we are weary, helping us handle challenges and find peace.

Weekly Summary:

This week, teens learned practical ways to balance the demands of school, friendships, and faith. By setting priorities, managing their time effectively, making faith a daily priority, recognizing a purpose in every season, and relying on God's strength, they can find a rhythm that keeps God at the center. Life's busyness can feel overwhelming, but with God's help, they can find peace and order.

Journaling Questions for Mentor:

1. What role does rest play in your spiritual life, and how do you prioritize time with God amidst daily responsibilities?

2. Reflect on a time when you had to make a difficult decision to put God first. How did it impact the other areas of your life?

3. How has relying on God's strength helped you handle seasons of busyness? Are there any areas where you are still learning to lean on Him?

4. Consider the areas in your life that require balancing right now. How can you take practical steps to manage them with God's wisdom?

5. Reflecting on Bethany Hamilton's story, what have you learned about trusting God to find balance during challenging times?

Real-Life Story:

Bethany Hamilton: Finding Balance Through Faith

One of the most powerful moments of Bethany Hamilton finding peace amidst chaos happened right after her shark attack in 2003. Bethany, a 13-year-old competitive surfer, was attacked by a 14-foot tiger shark while surfing off the coast of Hawaii, losing her left arm in an instant. The traumatic event not only threatened her life but also put her surfing dreams in jeopardy.

In the hospital, as she faced the gravity of her injury, Bethany was overwhelmed with fear and uncertainty. Yet, she turned to God, praying for strength and comfort. Amidst the chaos, she felt an unexplainable sense of peace and purpose. Bethany leaned on the Bible verse *"I can do all things through Christ who strengthens me"* (Philippians 4:13), which became her anchor during recovery.

With this peace guiding her, she returned to surfing just a month after the attack, learning to balance and ride the waves with one arm. Her resilience and unwavering faith inspired people around the world, showing that even in the face of incredible loss and chaos, peace and strength can be found through Jesus. This tragedy didn't stop her from pursuing her dreams of surfing competitively, and today, despite her busy schedule of surfing, competitions, and public speaking, she remains committed to her faith. Bethany often shares that finding balance starts with making God the center of everything: "When you put God first, everything else falls into place" (Hamilton, 2004). Her story encourages us to seek God's help in balancing life's responsibilities and to find peace in making time with the Lord a priority.

Discussion or Activity with Teen:

Activity:

When meeting with the teen this week, bring a little bit of chaos and intentional stress. Change the plan at the last minute. Have intentional interruptions during your time together, phone calls, errands you have to run, etc. Be intentionally distracted during this time. Then after a little stressful chaos, arrive at a destination where you can apologize for the acting and get serious and talk about how planning ahead and creating a schedule can remove stress and empower us to face the responsibilities of each day with confidence and peace. Planning is better than reacting.

or

"Creating a Balanced Weekly Plan"

1. Identify Key Areas: Help the teen list out their main responsibilities and commitments, such as schoolwork, extracurricular activities, friendships, family time, and personal faith practices (like prayer or Bible study).

2. Set Priorities: Ask them to rank these areas based on what they feel should be the top priorities for their well-being and growth, encouraging them to place God and personal time with Him high on the list.

3. Design a Weekly Plan: Using a calendar or planner, have them map out a typical week, ensuring that each important area has dedicated time. They should add a few minutes each day for prayer, Bible reading, or quiet time, making sure God remains at the center of their schedule.

4. Reflection and Adjustments: Encourage them to evaluate the plan after a week. Ask questions like: "Did the plan help you feel balanced? Were there areas where you needed more or less time?" Adjust the schedule as needed to keep it practical and realistic.

Debrief: Discuss how keeping God as a priority can bring calm and direction, even with a busy schedule. Emphasize that plans may need flexibility but keeping God at the center helps guide all their decisions.

Conversation Starter:

"How Can You Keep God at the Center of a Busy Schedule?"

Begin by asking about their typical day-to-day activities:

- "What takes up most of your time during the week?"

- "How do you currently make time for God in your day?"

- "What would make it easier to stay connected to God, even when you're busy?"

This conversation can help them consider specific ways to bring faith into their routine, showing them that prioritizing God isn't about perfection but about inviting Him into every area of life.

WEEK 27

STAYING PURE IN HEART AND MIND

Introduction:

This week's devotion focuses on purity, a theme that encourages teens to align their hearts and minds with God's standards in an often challenging culture. As you journey through this week with your teen, share your own experiences with maintaining purity, not just in actions but in thought and intention. Help them understand that purity goes beyond rules; it's about a heart transformed by God's love and a mind set on honoring Him.

Practical Challenge:

Teen Challenge: Choose one area of your life where you need to practice purity, whether it's in your thoughts, media choices, or actions. Make a commitment this week to guard your heart, seek God's help in overcoming temptation, and live in a way that honors Him.

Mentor Challenge: Consider an area in your life where you may need to renew your commitment to purity, whether in thoughts, media consumption, or daily habits. Set a specific goal for this week, perhaps choosing to limit certain influences or dedicating time for reflection and prayer. Invite God to purify your heart and align your thoughts with His. Encourage the teen in their challenge and pray for them.

Bible Story: Joseph Resisting Temptation (Genesis 39:6-12)

Reflection: Joseph's story offers a powerful example of purity and integrity. When tempted by Potiphar's wife, Joseph remained faithful to God, fleeing from the situation rather than compromising his values. His actions were motivated not just by the fear of consequences but by his commitment to honor God. Joseph's decision to prioritize purity, even at a great personal cost, shows us the importance of remaining steadfast in our convictions.

Key Themes:

- Choosing Purity: Joseph's story teaches us to choose purity even when no one is watching, trusting that God sees and honors our faithfulness.

- Fleeing Temptation: Sometimes purity requires physically or mentally removing oneself from situations that might lead to compromise.

- Faithfulness over Convenience: Joseph's commitment to God's standard reminds us that purity is about a deep, personal faithfulness rather than mere rule-following.

Teen Devotional Recap:

- **Day 1:** *Why Purity Matters to God* – Matthew 5:8 – A pure heart draws closer to God, allowing us to reflect His holiness in our lives and relationships.

- **Day 2:** *Guarding Your Heart Against Negative Influences* – Proverbs 4:23 – Guarding your heart by being mindful of influences helps protect you from harmful distractions and keeps you grounded in God's truth.

- **Day 3:** *Maintaining Purity in What You Watch, Read, and Listen To* – Philippians 4:8 – Choosing uplifting and God-honoring media supports a mindset aligned with purity and keeps the heart focused on what is good.

- **Day 4:** *Overcoming Temptations Through Prayer and Scripture* – 1 Corinthians 10:13 – Temptation is universal, but God is faithful, always providing strength and a way out when we seek Him.

- **Day 5:** *Developing Pure Thoughts and Actions* – Psalm 51:10 – Asking God for a pure heart leads to transformed desires and actions that honor Him.

Weekly Summary:

This week, teens learned about purity as a lifestyle that starts in the heart. By understanding why purity matters to God, guarding their hearts, choosing uplifting media, relying on prayer, and pursuing a pure mindset, they can walk closely with Him. Staying pure is more than avoiding certain behaviors; it's about growing in a relationship with God that influences their actions and brings glory to Him.

Journaling Questions for Mentor:

1. Reflect on a time when you struggled with purity, whether in thoughts, actions, or influences. How did you see God working to draw you back to Him?

2. In what ways do you guard your own heart and mind, and how can you encourage your teen to do the same?

3. Consider a time when you felt the need to remove yourself from a tempting situation. How did choosing purity impact your relationship with God and others?

4. What habits or influences have you found helpful for keeping your thoughts and actions focused on God?

5. How has God renewed your desires over time, helping you to seek what is pure and pleasing to Him?

Real-Life Story:

Elisabeth Elliot: Pursuing Purity of Heart and Mind

Elisabeth Elliot, a missionary, author, and speaker, was known for her commitment to living a life of purity and holiness. Elisabeth chose and championed purity while waiting to marry Jim Elliot by embracing a deep commitment to God's timing and principles. She and Jim met in college and had a strong connection and desire to marry, but Jim felt called to remain single at the time and move to the mission field in Ecuador, not knowing whether God would give him the freedom to marry later on. During this period, Elisabeth remained faithful to her Christian beliefs, focusing on spiritual growth, prayer, and trusting that God would lead them in the right direction. She upheld the values of purity and patience, believing that God's will was more important than their immediate desires. She once said, "Holiness has never been the driving force of the majority. It is, however, mandatory for anyone who wants to enter the kingdom" (Elliott, 1989, *Gate of Splendor*). Elisabeth and Jim did finally marry, and when they did, their relationship was built on a foundation of shared faith, trust in God's timing, and mutual commitment to purity. Elisabeth's life reminds us that living a pure life is about pursuing God above all else (Elliot, 2003).

Discussion or Activity with Teen:

Activity:

Sit together and brainstorm ways to maintain purity in various areas of life, including thoughts, media, friendships, and daily routines. Write down a list of "purity affirmations" or Scriptures that reinforce positive choices. These can be posted somewhere visible as daily reminders for both of you to strive for a heart and mind that honor God. If you think it is appropriate and applicable this might be a good time to have an honest conversation about pornography as statistically 4 of 5 teenage boys have been exposed. Be prepared to explain God's heart on the issue as well as the negative effects of pornography, individually, in relationships, and in society. Also be prepared to offer help and accountability.

or

"Media Reflection Challenge"

1. Media Review: Ask the teen to take note of the media they consume throughout the week—music, TV shows, movies, social media, and other content. They should write down any recurring themes they notice, such as language, messages about relationships, values, and so on.

2. Personal Reflection: Have them reflect on the impact of these themes. Ask them to consider questions like, "How does this content make me feel?" or "Does this bring me closer to or further from the mindset of purity God desires for me?"

3. Choose a Media Fast: Challenge them to take a break from one or two media sources that don't align with a pure mindset. During this break, encourage them to replace that time with positive, uplifting alternatives, like listening to worship music, reading a faith-based book, or spending time in prayer.

4. End-of-Week Reflection: At the end of the week, discuss how they felt during this media fast. Did they notice a difference in their mood, thoughts, or relationship with God?

Debrief: Talk about how the media we consume shapes our thoughts and hearts. Reinforce that choosing uplifting media is one way of guarding their heart and living out purity in everyday life.

Conversation Starter:

"What Does Purity Mean to You?"

Start the conversation with open questions to explore their understanding and personal views on purity:

- "When you think of purity, what comes to mind?"

- "What do you think it means to live a pure life that honors God?"

- "How can we make choices in our daily lives that reflect our desire to stay close to God?"

This can lead to discussing practical ways to make purity a positive and ongoing journey that strengthens their relationship with God.

WEEK 28

BODY IMAGE AND SELF-ESTEEM

Introduction:

This week's focus on body image and self-esteem can resonate deeply for teens and adults alike. In a world where society often emphasizes physical appearance over character, this devotional encourages looking beyond outward looks to see our true worth in Christ. Take time to reflect on your own experiences with body image and self-worth, and consider how you can model a Christ-centered perspective of value that is based on character, faith, and inner beauty. Your vulnerability and encouragement can help teens embrace the truth of who they are in God's eyes.

Practical Challenge:

Teen Challenge: Write down three qualities that God values in you that are not related to your appearance. Focus on developing these qualities throughout the week and remind yourself that your worth comes from God, not from how you look.

Mentor Challenge: This week, commit to focusing on character and qualities that reflect God's values rather than appearance. Write down three ways you can nurture inner qualities like kindness, patience, or faithfulness. Consider sharing these insights with your teen, showing them that true beauty and worth come from within.

Bible Story: David's Anointing (1 Samuel 16:6-13)

Reflection: When Samuel went to anoint the next king of Israel, he looked at David's older brothers and assumed that one of them, based on their appearance, would be chosen. But God rejected them, explaining to Samuel that He doesn't look at outward appearance but at the heart. Ultimately, God chose David, a young shepherd who had a heart for Him. This story highlights that God values the heart and character over physical appearance.

Key Themes:

- God's Perspective: God doesn't judge by appearance but by what's inside. This perspective challenges us to value character over outward looks.

- Chosen for Who We Are: God chose David not because he looked like a king, but because his heart sought after God.

- True Worth: David's worth and purpose were determined by God, not by society's standards or expectations.

Teen Devotional Recap:

- **Day 1:** *Understanding That You Are Made in God's Image* – Genesis 1:27 – Being made in God's image means you reflect His love and creativity. Your worth is rooted in God's design, not in appearance.

- **Day 2:** *Rejecting Society's False Standards of Value in Physical Appearance* – 1 Samuel 16:7 – The world focuses on outward looks, but God values what's in the heart. Seek to honor God by nurturing qualities like kindness, compassion, and faithfulness.

- **Day 3:** *Learning to Love and Care for Your Body* – 1 Corinthians 6:19-20 – Treating your body as a temple of the Holy Spirit shows respect for God's creation and honors Him through health and well-being.

- **Day 4:** *Focusing on Your Character, Not Just Appearance* – 1 Samuel 13:14 – God values a heart that follows Him, like David's. Focus on growing in character and seek to be someone after God's own heart.

- **Day 5:** *Finding Self-Esteem in God's Approval, Not Others* – Galatians 1:10 – True confidence comes from seeking God's approval rather than striving to meet society's standards or gain others' approval.

Weekly Summary:

This week's devotion reminded teens that they are created in God's image and that their worth is based on who God says they are, not on societal expectations or physical appearance. By focusing on character, caring for their bodies, and grounding their self-esteem in God's approval, they can develop a healthy view of themselves that reflects God's love and purpose.

Journaling Questions for Mentor:

1. Reflect on a time when you felt pressure to fit a certain appearance or standard. How did God guide you to see yourself through His eyes?

2. How can you guard your heart and mind from comparing yourself to others or feeling defined by society's standards of beauty?

3. In what ways can you model a healthy and God-honoring approach to body image and self-worth for the young people in your life?

4. How has seeking God's approval over people's approval changed your self-esteem and confidence over time?

5. What specific qualities or strengths has God developed in you that have nothing to do with physical appearance?

Real-Life Story:

Samantha Ponder: Finding True Beauty and Worth in Christ

Samantha Ponder's journey toward valuing her character and inner beauty more than external appearances began during her time in college. Like many young women, she faced the pressures of societal standards regarding beauty and success, particularly in the competitive world of sports media. She often felt the weight of expectations to look a certain way and to be perfect on camera.

One pivotal moment came during her internship with ESPN, where she was eager to impress and make a name for herself. She found herself in a high-pressure environment, surrounded by established professionals and facing criticism about her appearance. In the midst of trying to fit into this world, Samantha began to lose sight of who she truly was and what she valued most. Feeling disheartened, she turned to her faith for guidance. In prayer and reflection, Samantha began to understand that her worth was not defined by how others perceived her or by her physical appearance. She realized that her character, kindness, and authenticity were far more valuable than any external validation. This revelation sparked a transformation in her approach to her career and life.

Samantha began to focus on being genuine and uplifting rather than conforming to the pressures of the industry. She shared her faith openly, emphasizing the importance of inner strength and resilience. Her confidence grew as she recognized that her true beauty came from being a person of integrity, compassion, and faith. Through her platform, Samantha now encourages others to embrace their worth based on character rather than external appearances. She uses her voice to advocate for authenticity and self-acceptance, inspiring countless individuals to prioritize their inner beauty and to find strength in their identity as valued children of God (Sharp, 2024).

Discussion or Activity with Teen:

Activity:

Sit together and write down qualities that you each admire in someone close to you that have nothing to do with appearance. Share these qualities with each other and discuss why they are more meaningful than looks. You can also brainstorm ways to cultivate these qualities in your own lives as a reminder that inner character is what truly lasts and reflects God's heart. At the same time, pick a physical challenge that you and your teen can do together to honor the temple of the Holy Spirit. Consider hiking, running, lifting weights, or cutting out fast food and unhealthy snacks.

or

"Mirror Messages"

1. Write Positive Affirmations: Provide the teen with sticky notes or paper. Encourage them to write down five affirmations that reflect their worth in God's eyes. Examples include:

   ○ "I am fearfully and wonderfully made."

   ○ "God created me with purpose."

   ○ "I am loved and valued just as I am."

   ○ "My worth comes from God, not from appearances."

2. Place the Affirmations on a Mirror: Have them place these affirmations on their bathroom mirror or somewhere they will see them daily. Each time they look in

the mirror, they can be reminded of their true worth.

3. Daily Reflection: Encourage them to spend a few moments each day reflecting on one affirmation, praying for God's help to see themselves through His eyes.

Debrief: At the end of the week, discuss if these affirmations have impacted how they see themselves and if there's been a change in their self-esteem or confidence.

Conversation Starter:

"What Does It Mean to Be Made in God's Image?"

Share any struggles you currently have or have had with self esteem and then begin with questions to help them reflect on their unique worth:

- "When you hear that you're made in God's image, how does that make you feel about yourself?"

- "What are some unique qualities God has given you that have nothing to do with appearance?"

- "How can knowing your worth in God change the way you respond to societal pressures about looks?"

This conversation can lead to discussing practical ways to focus on character and inner beauty rather than external standards.

WEEK 29

DEALING WITH FAILURE

Introduction:

This week's theme of dealing with failure can be a meaningful opportunity to reflect on how God uses our mistakes and setbacks to grow us in ways we might never have anticipated. Teens often experience intense pressure to succeed, so discussing failure as part of God's plan for growth can be freeing. Encourage your teen to embrace their failures as learning opportunities and to lean into God's grace and strength when they fall short. By sharing your own experiences with failure and what you learned, you can help them see that they are not alone on this journey.

Practical Challenge:

Teen Challenge: Choose one past failure or mistake and pray for God's wisdom and grace to move forward from it. Ask Him to show you what you can learn from it and how you can use it as an opportunity for growth.

Mentor Challenge: Identify a past failure that still impacts you. Write down three lessons you learned from it and thank God for how He has used that experience to help you grow. Share this experience with your teen to encourage them to see setbacks as part of God's loving work in their lives.

Bible Story: Peter's Denial and Restoration (John 18:15-27; John 21:15-19)

Reflection: Peter's failure in denying Jesus three times was a moment of deep regret and shame for him. However, Jesus used this failure as a catalyst for Peter's restoration and growth. After His resurrection, Jesus met with Peter and gently asked him three times, "Do you love me?" This restored Peter's relationship with Jesus and reaffirmed his calling to shepherd others. Peter's failure didn't disqualify him; instead, Jesus turned it into a powerful opportunity for growth and ministry.

Key Themes:

- God's Grace in Failure: Jesus did not abandon Peter but instead offered him grace and restoration.

- Growth Through Setbacks: Peter's experience humbled him and prepared him to be a compassionate leader.

- A New Beginning: God often uses failure to open doors to greater maturity and purpose.

Teen Devotional Recap:

- **Day 1:** *Understanding That Failure Is Part of Life* – Proverbs 24:16 – Failure happens to everyone. God views failure as an opportunity for growth and resilience, not as the end of the story.

- **Day 2:** *How to Learn from Your Mistakes* – James 1:5 – Mistakes can teach us valuable lessons. Ask God for wisdom to help you see what you can learn and how you can grow.

- **Day 3:** *God's Grace When We Fail* – 2 Corinthians 12:9 – God's grace is sufficient, and He meets us in our weaknesses. We don't have to be perfect; God's love carries us through our failures.

- **Day 4:** *Moving Forward After Failure* – Philippians 3:13-14 – Rather than staying stuck in past mistakes, God calls us to move forward, pressing on to what He has ahead.

- **Day 5:** *Turning Failure into an Opportunity for Growth* – Romans 5:3-4 – Failure, when surrendered to God, can develop endurance, character, and hope within us.

Weekly Summary:

This week, teens learned that failure is a normal part of life and doesn't have to define them. Through God's grace, they can learn from their mistakes, move forward, and use failure as a tool for growth. Each failure is an opportunity to draw closer to God, lean on His strength, and develop character.

Journaling Questions for Mentor:

1. Reflect on a significant failure you've experienced. What lessons did God teach you through it?

2. How has failure helped you grow in your faith or reliance on God's strength and grace?

3. What words of encouragement would you offer to a young person who feels defined by a mistake?

4. How can you model resilience and hope for your teen when it comes to handling setbacks?

5. What specific areas of your life do you still need to surrender to God when it comes to fear of failure?

Real-Life Story:

Walt Disney: Failure as a Stepping Stone to Success

Early in his career, Disney faced numerous setbacks and challenges that could have derailed him. After moving to Hollywood in the 1920s, he launched a series of animation studios, but his first company, Laugh-O-Gram Studio, went bankrupt. Faced with failure, Disney had to start over, but he remained determined to pursue his passion for animation. In 1923, he and his brother Roy founded the Disney Brothers Studio, which later became The Walt Disney Company.

Despite his eventual success, Disney faced many obstacles along the way, including struggles with finances, creative disagreements, and the loss of his beloved character Oswald the Lucky Rabbit, who was taken from him by his distributor. However, instead of giving up, he created a new character—Mickey Mouse—who would go on to become an iconic figure in animation and entertainment. Reflecting on the value of failure in his life, Disney once said, "I think it's important to have a good hard failure when you're young. I learned a lot from that. I'm still learning" (Greene, 2016).

Throughout his career, Disney maintained a strong Christian faith, which provided him with hope and resilience during difficult times. His perseverance paid off as he revolutionized the animation industry and created beloved characters and theme parks that continue to bring joy to millions. Disney's journey is a testament to the idea that failure can lead to growth and unexpected success, inspiring countless people to pursue their dreams despite setbacks.

Discussion or Activity with Teen:

Activity:

Sit down with your teen and create a "Growth Chart" together, one for each of you. List past failures or challenges and the lessons learned from each one. Discuss how God used these experiences for growth, and celebrate the ways He has worked through your setbacks. This exercise can help your teen view failures as part of their journey rather than obstacles to their worth or success.

or

"Failure Reflections Journal"

1. Identify Past Challenges: Invite the teen to think of one or two failures or challenges they faced recently. These could be in school, friendships, sports, or personal goals.

2. Reflect on Lessons Learned: Have them write about each challenge, answering questions like:

   ○ What happened, and how did it make you feel?

   ○ What did you learn from the experience?

   ○ How did it change the way you see yourself or the situation?

   ○ How did it (or how could it) bring you closer to God?

3. Seek God's Perspective: Encourage them to pray, asking God to help them see the situation through His eyes. Afterward, they can jot down any insights or feelings of peace that come from their prayer.

4. End with Gratitude: Conclude with a sentence or two of gratitude for the experience and how it's shaping them, even if they don't fully understand it yet.

Debrief: At the end of the week, ask how this reflection impacted their view of failure and if they feel any closer to God or more hopeful about handling future challenges.

Conversation Starter:

"What Have You Learned Through Failing?"

After sharing your own experience with failure, use these questions to open a discussion on seeing failure positively:

- "Can you think of a time you felt like you failed at something but ended up learning from it?"

- "What's something you'd like to handle differently next time you face a setback?"

- "How does it feel to know that failure doesn't define you in God's eyes?"

This can lead to a meaningful conversation on how God uses every experience for growth, even those that feel like setbacks.

WEEK 30

BUILDING HEALTHY HABITS

Introduction:

This week's focus on building healthy habits is an excellent opportunity to discuss the importance of small, consistent choices that lead to spiritual growth. As teens navigate their busy schedules, they often find it challenging to prioritize spiritual disciplines, but developing habits that honor God can guide their daily lives. You can encourage your teen to start small, emphasize consistency, and remind them that even little actions can create big changes over time. Share personal examples of habits that have helped you grow in faith, and brainstorm together on practical ways they can cultivate similar habits.

Practical Challenge:

Teen Challenge: Pick one habit you'd like to develop this week, whether it's praying daily, reading the Bible each morning, listening to a biblical podcast, or speaking more kindly to others. Create a simple plan to stay consistent in this habit, and ask God for strength to stick with it.

Mentor Challenge: Identify one habit you would like to improve or build in your spiritual life this week, such as a regular time for prayer, reading Scripture, a dedicated time for worship, or connecting with others in fellowship. Set a small, achievable goal for each day, and invite your teen to join you. Use this as an opportunity to encourage each other, share what you're learning, and see how God works through your commitment.

Bible Story: Jesus' Habit of Prayer (Mark 1:35-39)

Reflection: Throughout His ministry, Jesus demonstrated the importance of building and maintaining habits, particularly the habit of prayer. In Mark 1:35-39, we see Jesus rising early in the morning to pray in a quiet place before starting His day of ministry. Even though He was surrounded by people needing His help, Jesus made prayer a priority, setting an example for us to seek God first. His commitment to regular prayer and time alone with God gave Him strength, guidance, and peace to fulfill His mission. This habit kept Him connected to the Father and helped Him stay focused on His purpose.

Key Themes:

- Prioritizing Time with God: Jesus modeled the importance of setting aside time to connect with God, regardless of how busy life may be.

- Consistency in Prayer: Jesus' habit of consistent prayer shows that a close relationship with God is built through regular, intentional time with Him.

- Empowerment Through Spiritual Discipline: Jesus' prayer habit empowered Him to stay focused, resist distractions, and fulfill His purpose. Similarly, spiritual habits empower us to grow closer to God and stay grounded in His will.

Teen Devotional Recap:

- **Day 1:** *How Small Habits Can Lead to Big Changes* – Luke 16:10 – Small, faithful actions can lead to significant growth and transformation over time.

- **Day 2:** *Developing Spiritual Habits Like Prayer and Bible Reading* – Psalm 1:2-3 – Consistent time in God's Word and prayer strengthens our faith, much like water nourishes a tree by a river.

- **Day 3:** *Creating Routines That Honor God* – 1 Timothy 4:7-8 – Training for godliness involves creating routines that reflect our values and honor God.

- **Day 4:** *Breaking Bad Habits with God's Help* – Colossians 3:8-10 – God gives us the strength to replace bad habits with godly habits that reflect our new nature in Christ.

- **Day 5:** *Staying Consistent in Building Healthy Habits* – Hebrews 12:11 – Developing good habits takes time and discipline, but it produces a harvest of peace and righteousness.

Weekly Summary:

This week, teens explored the importance of healthy habits by recognizing the power of small, consistent actions, committing to spiritual practices like prayer and Bible reading, creating routines that honor God, overcoming bad habits, and staying disciplined. Developing habits that reflect a commitment to God helps them grow in faith, build character, and experience His peace.

Journaling Questions for Mentor:

1. What small habits have you developed over the years that have helped you grow closer to God?

2. How has consistency in spiritual disciplines impacted your faith?

3. What routines can you incorporate into your week that reflect your desire to honor God?

4. Are there any habits that you feel called to change or improve with God's help?

5. How can you support your teen in developing and staying consistent in their own healthy habits?

Real-Life Story:

William Carey: Discipline and Perseverance in Daily Habits

William Carey, known as the "father of modern missions," was a missionary to India who displayed great discipline and commitment to daily habits that helped him achieve his God-given purpose. He dedicated his life to translating the Bible into multiple Indian languages, often working tirelessly despite many setbacks and challenges. Carey once said, "Expect great things from God; attempt great things for God" (Carey, 1792). His life shows how small, consistent habits of prayer, study, and discipline led to significant impact and growth in God's kingdom. Carey's example encourages us to develop healthy habits that honor God and contribute to His purpose for our lives.

Discussion or Activity with Teen:

Activity:

Choose a "Habit-Building Challenge" to do together with your teen. Decide on one habit you'd like to develop (such as daily prayer, reading a chapter of the Bible, practicing gratitude, or exercising) and make a plan to stay consistent each day for one week. Create a chart to track your progress, and at the end of the week, discuss what you learned and how God worked through your efforts. This exercise can be a fun way to encourage each other and see firsthand how small actions can lead to meaningful growth. After the week is over consider extending the challenge or taking up another habit-building challenge.

or

"Habit Tracker Challenge"

1. Choose a Habit: Ask the teen to select one healthy habit they'd like to work on this week. This could be a spiritual habit, like daily prayer or Bible reading, or something that contributes to their overall well-being, like exercising or speaking kindly to others.

2. Set a Goal and Track Progress: Provide a simple habit tracker — either a piece of paper with a weekly checklist or a digital habit-tracking app. Encourage them to check off each day they complete the habit.

3. Reflect Midweek: Around the middle of the week, check in to see how the habit is going. Ask them if they've encountered any challenges and if there's anything they can adjust to stay consistent.

4. End with Reflection: At the end of the week, have them review their progress and journal or pray about any positive changes they've noticed in their mindset or relationship with God.

Debrief: Encourage a conversation about how this small, consistent habit impacted their week and how committing to it helped them feel closer to God.

Conversation Starter:

"What's One Habit That Could Bring You Closer to God?"

After sharing about your journey to better habits, use these questions to start a meaningful discussion on healthy habits and spiritual growth:

- "If you could choose one new habit to strengthen your faith, what would it be?"

- "What makes it challenging to stick with good habits, and how do you think God can help?"

- "Have you ever noticed how little habits, good or bad, can make a big difference over time?"

This conversation can guide them to see that healthy habits are manageable with God's help and can make a big impact on their faith journey.

WEEK 31

SETTING GOALS WITH GOD IN MIND

Introduction:

Goal-setting is a valuable practice that encourages both growth and purpose. This week's focus on setting goals with God in mind is a reminder that while achieving personal milestones is rewarding, aligning goals with God's purpose brings lasting fulfillment. Teens may face pressures to succeed academically, socially, and personally. As a mentor, guide them in setting goals that honor God and encourage a heart willing to follow His leading, even when goals evolve. Share stories of times when God redirected your plans for a greater purpose, and be open about the blessings of following His guidance.

Practical Challenge:

Teen Challenge: Choose one goal to pray about this week, asking God for wisdom, direction, and timing. Write down small steps you can take toward achieving it, and be open to God's guidance and redirection along the way.

Mentor Challenge: Recall a past goal that you accomplished with the Lord's help and share that story with your teen or identify a personal goal you would like to set or revisit. Spend time in prayer, asking God to show you how this goal aligns with His purpose and direction for your life. Break the goal down into small, manageable steps, and ask God for the patience and discipline to pursue it in His timing. Share this journey with your teen, offering insights on the value of partnering with God in goal-setting.

Bible Story: Nehemiah's Goal-Setting and Dependence on God (Nehemiah 2:1-8)

Reflection: When Nehemiah felt called to rebuild the walls of Jerusalem, he set out with clear goals and careful planning, but he first sought God's guidance. Despite the risks, he remained prayerful, humble, and open to God's timing. Nehemiah understood that the success of his goal depended on God's favor, and he was willing to adjust and stay flexible based on God's direction.

Key Themes:

- Commitment to God's Purpose: Nehemiah's goal was rooted in a desire to honor God and serve his community.

- Planning with Faith: While he prepared well, Nehemiah depended on God's provision and timing.

- Openness to God's Guidance: Nehemiah adjusted his plans based on God's direction, modeling a balance of planning and faith.

Teen Devotional Recap:

- **Day 1:** *Why It's Important to Set Goals That Align with God's Will* – Proverbs 16:3 – Commit your goals to God, trusting Him to direct and establish your plans.

- **Day 2:** *Praying About Your Goals and Dreams* – Isaiah 28:29 – Bringing your goals to God in prayer invites His wisdom and guidance.

- **Day 3:** *Breaking Big Goals Into Manageable Steps* – Psalm 37:23 – Breaking goals into small steps helps you stay focused while allowing God to guide each step.

- **Day 4:** *Trusting God's Timing for Your Goals* – Ecclesiastes 3:11 – God's timing is perfect, even if it differs from our expectations.

- **Day 5:** *Being Flexible and Open to God's Redirection* – James 4:13-15 – Stay open to God's adjustments, knowing He may redirect for a greater purpose.

Weekly Summary:

This week, teens explored the importance of setting goals that align with God's will, praying for direction, breaking goals into achievable steps, trusting God's timing, and remaining flexible to His redirection. Goals are an essential part of growth, but God's guidance gives them lasting value and leads to true fulfillment.

Journaling Questions for Mentor:

1. How has seeking God's guidance in setting goals shaped your experiences and outcomes?

2. What are some goals you've set that God later redirected? How did this affect your faith and perspective?

3. How can you encourage your teen to be patient with God's timing, especially when goals seem delayed?

4. What small steps have helped you stay faithful to long-term goals, even when progress was slow?

5. In what ways can you support your teen in setting meaningful goals that reflect God's purpose?

Real-Life Story:

David Green: Setting Goals with God's Purpose in Mind

David Green, founder of Hobby Lobby, has built a successful business while keeping God at the center of his goals and decisions. Throughout his career, Green has remained committed to honoring God through his work and has sought God's guidance in every decision. He once said, "I just keep my eyes on Christ, and I try to keep my goals aligned with what He wants for my life" (Greene, 2017). Green's story is a reminder that when you set goals with God's purpose in mind, He will lead and bless your path.

Discussion or Activity with Teen:

Activity:

Goal-Setting Vision Board

Create a vision board with your teen to visualize goals they feel called to pursue. Use magazines, images, quotes, or Bible verses that inspire them to stay focused on God's plan for their lives. Discuss how each goal can be broken down into smaller steps and how to seek God's guidance for each part of their journey. Display the board somewhere visible as a reminder to pray for God's wisdom and direction regularly.

or

"Goal-Setting with God"

1. Identify a Goal: Encourage the teen to think of another goal they'd like to set or the same goal they have been working on this week, whether it's spiritual, academic, or personal. Have them write it down in a notebook or journal.

2. Pray Over the Goal: Guide them in praying over the goal, asking for God's wisdom, guidance, and alignment with His will. Emphasize the importance of listening for God's direction throughout the process.

3. Break It Down: Help them create 2–3 small, achievable steps they can take toward the goal in the next week. For instance, if their goal is to increase their grade in Science by the end of the semester, the steps might include breaking the semester down into future assignments and tests and setting aside a specific amount of time each day to work on those assignments or prepare for the tests or seeking peer tutoring in that subject.

4. Reflect and Adjust: Encourage the teen to check in at the end of the week to see how they did with each step. Ask them if they feel God leading them to adjust the goal or add any new steps.

Debrief: Have them share how trusting God with their goal helped them stay focused and whether any changes or redirections felt like guidance from God.

Conversation Starter:

"How Do You Invite God into Your Goals?"

After sharing something from your own journey with goal setting, use these questions to discuss aligning goals with God's will:

- "When you think about setting goals, how often do you consider what God wants for you?"

- "Why do you think it's important to invite God into your planning and decision-making?"

- "What's one way you can trust God's timing with a goal you're working toward?"

This discussion can help the teen see that goals aligned with God's will lead to deeper fulfillment and peace.

WEEK 32

DEVELOPING A GRATEFUL HEART

Introduction:

Gratitude is a powerful response to God's goodness, transforming how we view both blessings and challenges. This week, encourage your teen to see gratitude as more than just a feeling but as an intentional choice that brings perspective and peace, even during hardship. Share how gratitude has impacted your life, especially in difficult seasons, and walk alongside them as they discover the joy and strength that comes from a grateful heart.

Practical Challenge:

Teen Challenge: Start a gratitude journal this week, writing down at least three things you're thankful for each day. Reflect on God's goodness, and let gratitude fill your heart, even in the midst of challenges.

Mentor Challenge: Start your own gratitude journal this week, listing at least three things you're thankful for each day. Share a few of these with your teen, and encourage them to join you in recording their gratitude. This simple habit can open your hearts to recognize God's daily faithfulness and inspire you both to live with joy and contentment.

Bible Story: Paul and Silas's Gratitude in Prison (Acts 16:22-26)

Reflection: When Paul and Silas were wrongfully imprisoned, they chose to respond with prayer and songs of worship rather than despair. In the middle of the night, as they praised God, a miraculous earthquake freed them from their chains. Their choice to be grateful and focus on God's power, even in suffering, not only brought personal peace but also led to the transformation of the jailer and his family. Paul and Silas's story reminds us that gratitude, even in dark times, has a ripple effect, bringing hope and encouragement to others.

Key Themes:

- Choosing Gratitude in Trials: Paul and Silas's response shows that gratitude can exist even in the worst circumstances.

- God's Power Through Praise: Their gratitude and worship became a catalyst for God's miraculous intervention.

- The Impact of Gratitude on Others: Gratitude and joy are contagious and can draw others to God's love.

Teen Devotional Recap:

- **Day 1:** *Keeping a Gratitude Journal to Remind Yourself of God's Goodness* – Psalm 103:2 – A gratitude journal helps remind us of God's faithfulness.

- **Day 2:** *How to Focus on Blessings Instead of Problems* – Psalm 107:1-2 – Focusing on blessings over problems brings positivity and joy.

- **Day 3:** *The Importance of Gratitude in Daily Life* – 1 Thessalonians 5:18 – Gratitude changes our perspective, even in hard times.

- **Day 4:** *Learning to Give Thanks Even in Difficult Situations* – 1 Peter 4:12-13 – Gratitude in challenges builds faith, knowing God is at work.

- **Day 5:** *How Gratitude Brings Joy and Contentment* – Colossians 3:15 – Gratitude fills us with joy, contentment, and peace.

Weekly Summary:

This week, teens explored how to develop a grateful heart by keeping a gratitude journal, focusing on blessings, choosing gratitude daily, giving thanks in hard times, and finding joy and contentment through a thankful spirit. Gratitude can transform any season, bringing peace, perspective, and a deeper awareness of God's love.

Journaling Questions for Mentor:

1. How has gratitude changed your outlook on challenging situations in your life?

2. In what ways can you model gratitude for your teen, especially during difficult times?

3. Is there an area where you struggle with gratitude? How can you ask God to help you see His goodness in that situation?

4. How has keeping a gratitude journal, if you've tried it, helped you recognize God's blessings more fully?

5. How can you encourage your teen to focus on gratitude daily, even when life feels overwhelming?

Real-Life Story:

Corrie ten Boom: Gratitude in the Midst of Suffering

Corrie ten Boom, a survivor of a Nazi concentration camp and author of *The Hiding Place*, understood the power of gratitude in difficult circumstances. She and her sister Betsie were imprisoned for hiding Jews during World War II, yet they chose to give thanks even while suffering. One day, they thanked God for the fleas infesting their barracks, only to later find out that the fleas kept the guards away, allowing them to hold Bible studies in secret. Corrie's life shows that gratitude can be found even in the darkest times, and God uses all things for His glory (Ten Boom, 1974).

Discussion or Activity with Teen:

Activity:

Find an activity to do together such as a walk, hike, or miniature golf. While you are together, have a gratitude competition. Each one of you takes a turn saying something you are grateful for. The first one that can't come up with something within 10 seconds loses. Then have a real discussion about how good God is in each of your lives. Take a few minutes to express that gratitude to God.

or

Gratitude Jar

Create a "Gratitude Jar" together, where each of you can write down things you're thankful for on slips of paper. Throughout the week, fill the jar with notes of gratitude — for answered prayers, simple joys, or people who have impacted your life. At the end of the week (or month), read through the slips together and reflect on God's blessings. This can become a cherished routine that reminds you both of God's faithfulness and the importance of gratitude.

Conversation Starter:

"How Has Gratitude Changed You?"

After sharing a little of your own experience with gratitude, use these questions to discuss the impact of gratitude:

- "What's one thing you wrote down in your gratitude journal that surprised you or that you don't usually think about?"

- "How do you feel when you focus on gratitude, even in tough times?"

- "How do you think being thankful can help you get closer to God or grow in faith?"

This conversation can help the teen understand that gratitude is a powerful tool for seeing God's presence in every season.

WEEK 33

MANAGING TIME WISELY

Introduction:

In today's fast-paced world, managing time wisely can feel challenging, especially for teens who are balancing school, friendships, activities, and their relationship with God. This week, your role as a mentor is to guide them in seeing time as a gift from God and to help them develop habits that honor Him. Share your own experiences with time management and the lessons you've learned along the way.

Practical Challenge:

Teen Challenge: Make a list of all of your activities this week. Then go back and number those activities with a number between 1 and 5. 1 signifies that the activity has no importance in the Kingdom of God and 5 means the activity is very important in the Kingdom of God. After you complete this task, consider what things you can take out of your schedule to make God's Kingdom a higher priority as far as how you actually spend your time.

Mentor Challenge: This week, consider completing the practical challenge alongside your teen. List your activities and evaluate them based on their eternal significance, just as your teen will be doing. Discuss any activities you're both considering changing or reprioritizing, and talk about how time spent on Kingdom-focused activities can make a lasting impact.

Bible Story: The Parable of the Stewards – Matthew 25:14-30

Reflection: In the Parable of the Stewards (also known as the Parable of the Talents), Jesus tells the story of a master who entrusts his property to three servants before going on a journey. He gives each servant a different amount of money (talents) according to their ability. The first two servants wisely invest their talents, doubling the master's money. But the third servant, out of fear, buries his talent in the ground and fails to use it. When the master returns, he praises the first two servants for their faithfulness and rewards them with greater responsibilities. However, he rebukes the third servant for his laziness and lack of initiative, taking away the talent and giving it to the one who has the most.

This parable highlights the importance of using our time, resources, and abilities wisely. God has given each of us unique gifts and opportunities, and He calls us to be faithful stewards of these blessings. Our goal should not be to compare ourselves to others but to invest what we've been given to bring glory to God. When we manage our time and talents well, we honor God and experience growth and purpose.

Key Themes:

- **Faithfulness with Resources:** The parable emphasizes that each of us is responsible for how we use what God has entrusted to us. Faithfulness means making the most of what we have, no matter the amount, and seeking to grow and improve.

- **Taking Initiative and Avoiding Fear:** The third servant allowed fear to prevent him from taking action. Jesus teaches us not to let fear stop us from using our gifts and taking risks for the kingdom. God desires that we act in faith, trusting Him to guide us.

- **Accountability and Reward:** The master held each servant accountable for how they used their talents. Likewise, God values our efforts and will one day hold us accountable for how we managed what He has given us. Faithful stewardship brings rewards and greater responsibility.

Teen Devotional Recap:

- **Day 1:** *The Importance of Using Your Time for God's Glory* – Psalm 90:12 – Time is a precious gift; using it for God's glory brings wisdom.

- **Day 2:** *Identifying Time-Wasters and Distractions* – Romans 13:11 – Being mindful of distractions allows us to live purposefully.

- **Day 3:** *Learning to Prioritize Your Tasks* – Isaiah 46:10 – Prioritizing tasks in line with God's will makes our time meaningful.

- **Day 4:** *Making Time for Rest and Sabbath* – Mark 2:27 – Rest is a vital part of life that allows us to recharge and focus on God.

- **Day 5:** *Seeking God's Guidance on How to Use Your Time* – Romans 11:33 – Seeking God's wisdom guides us in managing time effectively.

Weekly Summary:

This week, teens explored managing time wisely by recognizing its value, identifying distractions, prioritizing tasks, making time for rest, and seeking God's guidance. Emphasize to your teen that wise time management is not just about getting more done but about making sure their time aligns with God's purpose.

Journaling Questions for Mentor:

1. How have you learned to manage your time over the years, and what has helped you align it with God's purposes?

2. Are there any time-wasters in your life that you can remove or reduce to focus on what's most important?

3. How can you encourage your teen to make time for rest and Sabbath, modeling a healthy balance of work and rest?

4. What ways do you seek God's guidance in managing your time, and how has this impacted your priorities?

5. Are there specific areas in your schedule where you feel God leading you to make a change? How can you adjust to align with His priorities?

Real-Life Story:

J.C. Penney: Using Time and Resources Wisely

J.C. Penney, the founder of the J.C. Penney retail chain, was a businessman who understood the importance of managing time and resources with God's guidance. In the early days of his business, Penney faced the pressures of running his stores and meeting the demands of an expanding retail empire. He often found himself working long hours, sometimes at the expense of his health and family life. However, he realized that success in business should not come at the cost of neglecting his loved ones or his personal well-being.

One significant turning point came after he faced a severe health crisis in the 1930s, which forced him to reevaluate his life. He had experienced a series of personal and financial challenges, including the death of his beloved wife and the stress of the Great Depression affecting his business. During this tumultuous time, Penney began to focus on how he was spending his time, choosing to prioritize what truly mattered: his faith, family, and the well-being of his employees. He made a conscious decision to allocate his time to activities that aligned with his values, such as attending church, spending quality moments with family, and engaging with the community. He began to implement practices in his business that emphasized the importance of work-life balance, encouraging his employees to do the same.

J.C. Penney's transformation not only improved his personal life but also positively influenced his business practices. He fostered a company culture that valued integrity, respect, and a commitment to service, which resonated with both his employees and customers. Ultimately, Penney's decision to prioritize his time wisely led to a legacy that went beyond retail success; it demonstrated the importance of living a balanced life centered on core values and meaningful relationships. His story continues to inspire many in both business and personal realms, reminding us that true success involves wise stewardship of our time and resources (Jones, 1971).

Discussion or Activity with Teen:

Activity:

Do a little research on how Messianic Jews celebrate Shabat and invite the teen for a Shabat dinner on Friday night. The rituals very from family to family but they all share the same principles. As a believer in Jesus, the primary point is to recognize that we can rest because of what Christ accomplished for us. A couple of key points to teach are that in the beginning God declared His creation of man was "good" before man had accomplished anything. The other is that for God, the day starts in the evening, when we are resting, so the day starts with rest and ends with work. That is the opposite of our thinking that the day starts with work in the morning and ends with rest in the evening. Let these subtle reminders bring you deeper into God's rest.

or

"Weekly Time Audit and Prioritization"

1. Time Inventory: Have the teen track their activities for one day or over a couple of days, noting how much time they spend on school, social media, hanging out with friends, family time, and other activities.

2. Evaluate and Categorize: Guide them to review their time use and categorize each activity as either:

   ○ High Priority (important for growth, relationships, or their faith journey),

   ○ Moderate Priority (necessary but could be reduced), or

   ○ Low Priority (distractions or activities with little lasting benefit).

3. Reordering for Growth: Challenge them to identify at least one "Low Priority" activity they could reduce or replace with a "High Priority" activity that aligns with their goals or God's purpose for them.

4. Weekly Planning: Encourage them to review the simple weekly plan from Week 26 , setting specific times for what matters most, such as homework, prayer, or family time. Remind them that rest is also an important priority!

Debrief: At the end of the week, talk with them about how it felt to manage their time intentionally and if they noticed any positive changes in their mood, stress level, or productivity.

Conversation Starter:

"What Does Using Time Wisely Look Like to You?"

Here are some questions to help the teen reflect on wise time management:

- "What's one activity that feels like a distraction in your week? How does it impact your time and focus?"

- "How do you think using your time well can help you grow closer to God?"

- "What's one change you could make in your schedule that would help you feel more balanced and purposeful?"

- Ask your teen to share what they rated as a "5" or "1" on their list of activities. Discuss why they gave each rating and how they can begin to adjust their schedule to reflect what matters most. This conversation can be a valuable time for both of you to reflect on your commitments and realign with what truly matters.

This conversation can help them see that managing time wisely isn't just about productivity but about aligning their time with their values and God's priorities.

WEEK 34

STAYING HUMBLE

Introduction:

Humility is a core virtue in the Christian life, yet it's often misunderstood. This week, you'll be guiding your teen through an exploration of humility — what it is, what it isn't, and why it matters so deeply to God. As you walk alongside them, encourage them to see humility as a strength rather than a weakness. Share moments from your life when humility allowed God to work more fully in and through you.

Practical Challenge:

Teen Challenge: Find a way to serve someone this week in humility, whether it's helping a friend, volunteering, or simply showing kindness to someone in need. Let your act of service be an expression of Christ's love and humility.

Mentor Challenge: Join your teen in this week's practical challenge by serving someone in humility. It could be a neighbor, a church member, or even a stranger. Reflect together on how the experience brought joy and deepened your faith. Look for ways to make service a regular practice in your lives, setting an example of humility.

Bible Story: Jesus Teaches on Humility — Matthew 23:1-12

Reflection: In Matthew 23:1-12, Jesus speaks to the crowds and His disciples about the Pharisees and teachers of the law, warning them not to follow their example of pride and hypocrisy. The Pharisees held positions of authority and loved the respect that came with it, yet they neglected the true heart of service. They performed religious acts to be seen by others, placing heavy burdens on people's shoulders without offering support or understanding. Jesus encouraged His followers to avoid this attitude, teaching that greatness in God's kingdom is found not in titles or recognition but in humble service to others. He said, "The greatest among you will be your servant. For those who exalt themselves will be humbled, and those who humble themselves will be exalted."

This passage challenges us to examine our motives and strive for true humility. Jesus reminds us that in God's eyes, genuine service is more valuable than outward displays of status. When we put others before ourselves and serve with a sincere heart, we reflect Jesus' love and show the world what it means to live with humility.

Key Themes:

- Humility Over Pride: Jesus warns against pride and self-importance, showing that true greatness comes from a humble heart willing to serve others without seeking recognition.

- Service as the Path to True Honor: Jesus teaches that honor in God's kingdom is given to those who serve selflessly. When we focus on helping others rather than elevating ourselves, we reflect His love and compassion.

- Avoiding Hypocrisy: Jesus calls out the Pharisees for their hypocrisy, urging His followers to practice what they preach. Genuine humility is about being authentic in our words and actions, letting our faith shape how we treat others.

Teen Devotional Recap:

- **Day 1:** *Why Humility Is a Key Christian Virtue* – Philippians 2:3-4 – Humility is about valuing others and thinking beyond our own interests.

- **Day 2:** *How Jesus Demonstrated Humility* – John 13:14-15 – Jesus' example of washing the disciples' feet shows humility in action.

- **Day 3:** *Recognizing Your Strengths Without Becoming Proud* – Romans 12:3 – Knowing your strengths without letting pride take root honors God.

- **Day 4:** *Serving Others as an Act of Humility* – Mark 10:45 – Serving others selflessly mirrors Christ's heart of humility.

- **Day 5:** *How to Accept Praise Without Letting It Inflate Your Ego* – 1 Corinthians 1:31 – Humility means directing praise and honor back to God.

Weekly Summary:

This week, your teen learned about the value of humility, how Jesus modeled it, how to serve others humbly, and how to handle praise without letting it lead to pride. Humility reflects Christ's character and strengthens relationships, creating a foundation for lasting joy and peace in Christ.

Journaling Questions for Mentor:

1. When was a time that choosing humility brought you closer to someone or helped you grow in your faith?

2. How do you keep your focus on serving God and others when it's easy to seek recognition or acknowledgment?

3. Have you seen a strength of yours become a point of pride? How did you work through that experience to give God the glory instead?

4. How has serving others shaped your perspective on humility and dependence on God?

5. How can you model humility to your teen, especially in areas where they might be prone to comparison or pride?

Real-Life Story:

Billy Graham: A Humble Heart for God

Billy Graham, one of the most well-known evangelists in history, was known not just for his preaching but also for his humility. Despite speaking to millions of people around the world, Graham always pointed the glory back to God. After one of his sermons, a prominent Hollywood producer approached him with an offer to film his crusades, which would significantly elevate his visibility and potentially lead to greater success. However, Graham was cautious and wanted to ensure that the focus remained on the message of Christ, not on himself. He politely declined the offer, feeling that it would detract from the gospel's central message.

Later, Graham was invited to meet with the producer and other influential figures in the entertainment industry. Instead of entering with an air of self-importance, he chose to approach the meeting with humility. He shared about his own shortcomings, how he was just a simple preacher called by God, and how his desire was to lead people to Christ rather than to gain fame or recognition. This humility resonated with those present, leaving a lasting impression on many who were used to the spotlight. Graham's approach not only exemplified his commitment to serving God above personal ambition but also helped build relationships with those who might have otherwise felt disconnected from the church.

Through moments like these, Billy Graham consistently demonstrated that true greatness comes from serving others and that humility is key to being an effective servant of Christ. His life remains a testament to the power of humility in leadership and ministry. He once said, "The ground is level at the foot of the cross, and I am just one of many who have been saved by God's grace" (Graham, 2006).

His humble heart and focus on serving others made a lasting impact, and his life is a powerful reminder that humility leads to greatness in God's kingdom.

Discussion or Activity with Teen:

Activity:

"Service in Secret"

1. Choose a Secret Act of Service: Encourage your teen to think of one or two things they can do for someone this week without seeking recognition. It could be helping a sibling with a chore, leaving an encouraging note for a friend, or doing something thoughtful for a family member.

2. Plan and Act: They should plan out how they'll carry out this act of service discreetly, making sure that they don't tell that person or others right away. This emphasizes the joy of serving humbly without seeking attention or acknowledgment.

3. Reflection on the Experience: After they've completed their act of service, ask them how it felt to serve without getting credit and how they think it impacted the other person. This helps them recognize the satisfaction of humility in action.

4. **NOTE:** The two of you could also plan to do some "secret service" together, creating twice as much fun.

Debrief: Discuss how doing things without praise or recognition can build character and bring a sense of peace, reminding them of Jesus' humble service.

or

Creating a "Service Journal"

Encourage your teen to start a simple service journal where they can record moments of service, humility, and gratitude. This could include times they felt humbled by helping others, received praise, or struggled with pride. Discuss what they learned from each experience and how they felt God's presence in those moments.

Conversation Starter:

"Why Does Humility Matter?"

Share a time when you struggled with pride or learned a lesson in humility. Ask your teen to consider how they handle praise or how they can keep their strengths in perspective. This open conversation can be a chance to grow together and support each other in choosing humility. Here are some questions to help your teen reflect on the role of humility:

- "Can you think of a time when being humble brought you closer to someone?"

- "Why do you think Jesus cared so much about humility? What did He show us through His actions?"

- "How do you feel when you do something good, and no one notices? How does it change when you remember that God sees everything?"

This discussion can open their eyes to the quiet strength of humility and how it builds trust and deepens their relationship with God.

WEEK 35

HONORING YOUR PARENTS

Introduction:

This week, your teen will be learning about the biblical command to honor their parents and how this reflects their relationship with God. They will explore ways to respect, appreciate, and serve their parents, even when there are disagreements. As a mentor, your role is to help your teen understand that honoring their parents is not just about obedience but also about showing love and respect, which pleases God. Encourage them to find practical ways to show honor and discuss the lifelong importance of this command, even as they gain independence.

Practical Challenge:

Teen Challenge: Choose one practical way to serve or appreciate your parents this week. Whether it's helping out around the house, writing a note of thanks, or spending quality time with them, find a way to honor them through your actions.

Mentor Challenge: (Same as the Teen Challenge) If your parents are no longer with you, choose someone you appreciate in your life to fulfill the challenge. Encourage your teen and at the end of the week, discuss how serving and honoring your parents has impacted your relationship with them.

Bible Story: Jesus Honoring His Mother, Even on the Cross (John 19:25-27)

Reflection: In John 19, we find Jesus, even in His final moments on the cross, showing care and honor to His mother, Mary. As He hung there, He looked down at His mother and the disciple John, and He instructed John to take Mary into his home and care for her as his own mother. This moment is significant because it shows that even in the midst of suffering, Jesus was concerned for His mother's well-being and took steps to ensure she would be cared for. Jesus' example teaches us that honoring our parents is not limited to childhood but is a lifelong commitment that continues in different forms as we grow older. It reminds us that honoring our parents reflects our love for them and our obedience to God's call.

Key Themes:

- Honoring parents is a lifelong commitment, not just a childhood responsibility.

- Caring for and respecting parents, even as we grow older, pleases God.

- Jesus provides the ultimate example of how we can honor our parents in all stages of life.

Teen Devotional Recap:

- **Day 1:** *Understanding the Biblical Command to Honor Parents* – Ephesians 6:2-3 – Honoring parents is a command from God that comes with the promise of blessing. It's not just about obedience but about showing respect and love to those who guide us.

- **Day 2:** *Showing Respect Even When You Disagree* – Colossians 3:20 – Even in disagreements, God calls us to honor our parents by respecting their perspective and speaking kindly. Honoring them doesn't mean we always agree, but it does mean treating them with respect.

- **Day 3:** *Practical Ways to Serve and Appreciate Your Parents* – Proverbs 23:22 – Honoring parents is shown through actions, such as helping around the house, listening to their advice, and showing appreciation for their care.

- **Day 4:** *How Honoring Your Parents Honors God* – Proverbs 1:8 – Honoring parents is a way of honoring God. Respecting their role in our lives and valuing their wisdom pleases God and reflects our obedience to His command.

- **Day 5:** *Balancing Independence with Respect as You Grow* – 1 Timothy 5:4 – Even as we gain independence, we are called to continue honoring and respecting our parents. Honoring them as adults means valuing their influence and showing them love throughout life.

Weekly Summary:

This week, your teen learned about the importance of honoring their parents as commanded by God. They explored how to show respect and appreciation, even in disagreements, and discovered that honoring parents is one way of honoring God. The teen also learned how to balance independence with respect as they grow older. As a mentor, encourage them to find practical ways to show love and respect to their parents this week, and help them understand that honoring parents is a lifelong commitment that reflects their faith.

Journaling Questions for Mentor:

1. Reflect on how you honored your parents growing up. How has that relationship changed as you've gained more independence?

2. How do you handle disagreements with your parents or elders in your life? How can you model respectful communication in those moments, both for your teen and for others?

3. What are some practical ways you can continue to honor and serve your parents, even as an adult? How can you share these practices with your teen to encourage them in their relationship with their parents?

4. How does honoring your parents reflect your relationship with God? What are some ways you can better show respect and love to those in authority in your life, such as parents, mentors, or elders?

5. How can you support your teen as they navigate the balance between growing independence and honoring their parents? What advice or experience can you share to help them honor their parents even when it's difficult?

Real-Life Story:

Jim Elliot: Honoring Parents Through Life's Decisions

Jim and Elisabeth Elliot were missionaries who served God faithfully in South America. Before they got married, Jim had to make a difficult decision — whether to obey God's call to missions or stay with his family, who were concerned for his safety. Jim valued his parents' input and sought to maintain open lines of communication. Rather than rebelling against their wishes, he took the time to explain his passion for missions and the call he felt from God. Jim also demonstrated his respect by considering their perspective and acknowledging their fears. Ultimately, Jim did follow the Lord's call and went into missions in South America; however, he continued to engage with his parents, showing them that he was making an informed and prayerful decision. His respectful approach reflected both his love for them and his dedication to his faith, highlighting the balance he sought between honoring his parents and following the Lord's calling. Even on the mission field later in life, both Jim and Elisabeth continued to honor their parents by sharing their journeys with them, praying for them, and valuing their wisdom (Elliot, 1989, *Shadow of the Almighty*).

Discussion or Activity with Teen:

Activity:

Take time to ask God together if there is anything your teen needs to ask forgiveness for in their relationship with their parents. Encourage your teen not to justify wrong actions because of their perception of their parents behavior, but to be honest before God and recognize when their actions or words were not showing honor. Then encourage your teen to either write a letter asking for forgiveness or, if they are comfortable, approach their parents in person to ask for forgiveness in person.

NOTE: If you are the parent of the teen, you need to really humble yourself and recognize your own faults in parenting. None of us are perfect parents. It is best if you set the example first, recognizing your mistakes and asking for forgiveness from your teen. There is no better way to demonstrate to them the teachings of Christ than this. If you really are not sure, ask your teen if you have ever offended them and give them space to answer honestly. I was 52 years old before I had to ask my adult children to forgive me for some things that I wished I had realized much sooner. The smallest things can become a wedge in your relationship when not dealt with, and sometimes that wedge is only seen through the other person's eyes.

or

"Acts of Appreciation"

1. **Create a List of Actions**: Ask your teen to brainstorm a list of small acts they can do to show appreciation for their parents. Examples could include helping with chores, writing a thank-you note, making them breakfast, or spending time with them.

2. **Choose One to Complete Each Day**: Encourage your teen to choose one action from their list each day this week and carry it out with a grateful heart. They don't need to mention they're intentionally honoring their parents — simply do it with a spirit of love.

3. **Reflection on the Experience**: At the end of the week, ask them to reflect on how it felt to show appreciation intentionally. Did they notice any changes in how they related to their parents?

4. **NOTE:** If you are the parent, let them keep this list secret, but be sure to praise them when they do things well. It might be best for this activity to save the praise until the end of the week so that they can have the experience of doing it for God first, but let the Lord lead you.

Debrief: Discuss how small acts of appreciation can strengthen relationships and honor God. Emphasize that honoring parents isn't just about obedience but showing love and gratitude.

Conversation Starter:

"What Does Honoring Your Parents Mean?"

Share some of your story, struggles and victories, in your relationship with your parents. Here are some questions to help your teen reflect on what honoring their parents looks like:

- "What does it mean to you to honor your parents? Can you think of specific ways you already do this?"

- "How do you handle disagreements with your parents while still showing them respect? What are some practical things you could do to balance those things better?"

- "Why do you think God asks us to honor our parents? What does it teach us about our relationship with Him?"

This conversation can help your teen explore the deeper reasons behind honoring parents, recognizing it as a reflection of their faith and a way to build stronger family relationships.

WEEK 36

RESPECTING AUTHORITY

Introduction:

This week, your teen will be learning about the importance of respecting authority figures. They will explore why God calls us to submit to leadership, how to disagree respectfully, and when it's appropriate to seek help if authority is misused. As a mentor, your role is to encourage your teen to see authority figures in their lives as people God has placed to guide and teach them. Respecting authority is a way to honor God and live in peace, but there's also a time to seek justice if authority is misused.

Practical Challenge:

Teen Challenge: This week, choose one authority figure in your life to show appreciation and respect for. It could be your teacher, coach, pastor, or another leader. Write them a note, say thank you, or find a way to express your gratitude for their leadership.

Mentor Challenge: (Same as the Teen Challenge) This week, choose one authority figure in your life to show appreciation and respect for. Whether it's your pastor, supervisor, or someone else in leadership, take the time to write them a note, say thank you, or express gratitude for their role in your life. Encourage your teen and at the end of the week, reflect together on how showing respect has strengthened your relationships with authority figures and discuss what it means to live with a culture of honor.

Bible Story: Daniel's Respect for Authority in a Foreign Land (Daniel 1:1-21)

Reflection: In Daniel 1, we see Daniel and his friends taken captive by the Babylonians and placed under the authority of a foreign king. Even in this challenging situation, Daniel showed respect for authority by cooperating with the officials. However, when it came to defiling himself by eating the king's food, Daniel respectfully requested an alternative that would honor God. Through his respectful approach, God gave Daniel favor, and he thrived under the king's authority without compromising his faith. Daniel's story teaches us that it's possible to respect authority while still standing firm in our convictions. His wisdom and respectful approach set an example for how we can honor authority figures while staying true to God's commands.

Key Themes:

- The importance of showing respect to those in authority, even when we don't fully agree.

- How to handle situations where authority conflicts with God's principles.

- The blessings that come when we honor God in how we approach authority.

Teen Devotional Recap:

- **Day 1:** *Why God Calls Us to Respect Authority Figures* – Romans 13:1 – God has placed authority figures in our lives for our good. Respecting them is not just about obeying rules but about honoring God's design for leadership and order.

- **Day 2:** *The Role of Teachers, Coaches, and Leaders in Your Life* – Hebrews 13:17 – Teachers, coaches, and pastors are placed in our lives to help us grow and learn. Respecting their role creates a culture of honor and makes their job a joy.

- **Day 3:** *How to Respectfully Disagree with Authority* – Proverbs 15:1 – Disagreeing with authority is sometimes necessary, but it should be done respectfully and with kindness. A gentle response can diffuse tension and build understanding.

- **Day 4:** *The Importance of Submitting to Authority When Appropriate* – Titus 3:1 – Submitting to authority helps us learn humility and discipline. It's about recognizing the order God has established and trusting His guidance through those He's placed over us.

- **Day 5:** *When to Seek Help if Authority is Abusive or Wrong* – Matthew 7:15-20 – While God calls us to respect authority, we should never tolerate abuse or wrongdoing. If authority is misused, it's important to seek help and stand for justice, reflecting God's heart for protection and care.

Weekly Summary:

This week, your teen learned about the importance of respecting authority figures and how God has placed leaders in our lives to guide us. They explored how to disagree respectfully, when to submit, and when to seek help if authority is misused. Respecting authority is a way to honor God, but standing for truth and justice is also necessary when authority is abused. Encourage your teen to see their teachers, coaches, and leaders as God-given sources of wisdom and to handle disagreements with grace and respect.

Journaling Questions for Mentor:

1. How has your understanding of authority changed as you've grown older? How can you model respect for authority figures in your life for your teen?

2. Reflect on a time when you had to respectfully disagree with someone in authority. How did you handle it, and what did you learn from the experience?

3. How can you show appreciation and respect for the leaders in your life, such as pastors, teachers, or supervisors? What are some practical ways you can encourage your teen to do the same?

4. How can submitting to authority help you grow in discipline and humility? How does this reflect your obedience to God?

5. Have you ever encountered a situation where authority was misused or abusive? How did you respond, and how can you guide your teen in seeking help when they face similar situations?

Real-Life Story:

Dietrich Bonhoeffer: Respecting Authority with Courage

Dietrich Bonhoeffer was a German pastor and theologian during World War II who respected authority but was also willing to stand up for what was right. In the early 1930s, as Hitler's government began to impose oppressive policies, Bonhoeffer was deeply troubled by the church's complicity in these actions. Many church leaders were either silent or supportive of the regime, but Bonhoeffer believed that Christians had a moral obligation to oppose evil.

In 1934, he attended a meeting of the German Evangelical Church, where discussions about the Nazi influence on the church were taking place. During the meeting, Bonhoeffer courageously spoke out against the state's encroachment into church affairs and the moral compromises that many church leaders were making. He respectfully confronted his colleagues, urging them to recognize the dangers of aligning with the Nazi government.

He famously said, "Silence in the face of evil is itself evil. God will not hold us guiltless. Not to speak is to speak. Not to act is to act" (Bonhoeffer, 2001). This quote encapsulated his conviction that Christians could not remain passive in the face of injustice.

Despite the risk of backlash from those in power, Bonhoeffer continued to advocate for the church to stand firm in its principles. He became involved in the Confessing Church movement, which sought to maintain the integrity of the Christian faith against Nazi ideology. As the situation in Germany worsened, Bonhoeffer's resistance intensified. Ultimately, Bonhoeffer was arrested in 1943 and executed in a concentration camp in 1945 for his opposition to the Nazi regime. His legacy as a courageous voice against tyranny and his refusal to remain silent in the face of evil continues to inspire people around the world to stand up for justice and truth (Metaxas, 2010).

Discussion or Activity with Teen:

Activity:

Choose some less obvious authority figures, such as the school principal, the local police, or the mayor. Choose one or more that you can both write a note to. Let them know you appreciate them and that you are praying for them. Then spend some time with your teen intentionally praying for God's wisdom and strength for those specific people in their roles of authority.

or

"Authority Appreciation"

1. **Identify Authority Figures**: Ask your teen to make a list of authority figures in their life (e.g., teachers, coaches, pastors, or leaders in the community).

2. **Choose Acts of Appreciation**: Encourage your teen to choose authority figures they feel particularly grateful for and show appreciation in a small, meaningful way. This could be writing a thank-you note, sending an email, or simply expressing appreciation in person.

3. **Reflection on Authority**: Afterward, have them reflect on how their chosen authority figures impact their life and why respecting authority is important in

the eyes of God.

Debrief: Discuss how showing appreciation can strengthen their relationship with authority figures. Emphasize that respect and gratitude for authority help build trust and also show a commitment to honoring God.

Conversation Starter:

"Respecting Authority While Honoring God"

Share any struggles you have had with authority in the past and how God helped you. Here are some questions to help your teen think through how they approach authority:

- "What does it mean to you to respect authority? Are there situations where it feels easier or harder to show respect?"

- "How do you handle disagreements with authority figures, like teachers or coaches? What are respectful ways to address those differences?"

- "Why do you think God calls us to respect authority? What can it teach us about our relationship with Him?"

This conversation can help your teen explore the balance between respecting authority and staying true to their beliefs. It's an opportunity to discuss that while respect is essential, God also values standing for truth, especially if they ever encounter misuse of authority.

Week 37

Choosing the Right Friends

Introduction:

This week, your teen will be focusing on the importance of choosing the right friends. The people we surround ourselves with have a significant impact on our decisions, character, and relationship with God. They will explore what makes a friendship godly and healthy, how to avoid toxic relationships, and the importance of being a good friend. Your role is to guide them in understanding that friendships are gifts from God, but they should be chosen wisely. Encourage them to think critically about their current relationships and how they can be a positive influence on their friends.

Practical Challenge:

Teen Challenge: Reach out to a friend who has been a positive influence in your life. Thank them for their friendship and encourage them in their faith. Make time to spend together, pray together, or simply catch up and support one another.

Mentor Challenge: This week, reach out to a close friend who has been a positive influence in your life. Take the time to thank them for their friendship and encourage them in their faith. Whether through a phone call, a handwritten note, or spending time together, make it a priority to strengthen your bond and support one another in your walk with God. Encourage your teen to do the same and discuss how godly friendships have impacted your lives.

Bible Story: Jonathan and David's Friendship (1 Samuel 18-20)

Reflection: The friendship between Jonathan and David is one of the most beautiful examples of a godly friendship in the Bible. Despite Jonathan being the son of King Saul, who sought to kill David, Jonathan remained loyal and protective of David. Their friendship was rooted in their mutual respect and love for God. Jonathan even sacrificed his own royal position to support David because he knew David was chosen by God. This story shows us the power of a friendship rooted in faith and loyalty. True friends love at all times, stand by each other through adversity, and encourage one another in the Lord. Jonathan and David's friendship is a model of how we should support, protect, and lift up our friends, especially when times are hard.

Key Themes:

- The importance of loyalty, trust, and mutual respect in friendships.

- How friendships rooted in God's love endure difficult circumstances.

- Sacrificing personal gain for the well-being of a friend and for God's plan.

Teen Devotional Recap:

- **Day 1:** *How Friends Influence Your Decisions and Character* – Proverbs 13:20 – Friends influence our character and decisions. Surrounding ourselves with wise, godly friends helps us grow in our faith, while negative influences can pull us away from God.

- **Day 2:** *What Makes a Friendship Healthy and Godly* – Proverbs 18:24 – A godly friendship is built on love, mutual support, and encouragement in faith. It's important to seek friends who lift us up and point us toward Christ.

- **Day 3:** *Signs of Toxic Friendships to Avoid* – 1 Corinthians 15:33 – Not all friendships are healthy. Toxic friends may lead us away from God, cause harm, or pressure us into poor decisions. Recognizing these friendships helps us set boundaries.

- **Day 4:** *The Value of Having Christian Friends* – Hebrews 10:24-25 – Christian friends encourage us, hold us accountable, and help us grow spiritually. Surrounding ourselves with believers strengthens our faith and provides support in difficult times.

- **Day 5:** *How to Be a Good Friend to Others* – Proverbs 27:6 – Being a good friend means loving others at all times, but also speaking truth with them and encouraging them to make better choices if necessary.

Weekly Summary:

This week, your teen learned about the powerful influence friends have on our lives and faith. They explored what makes a friendship godly, the importance of avoiding toxic relationships, and how to be a good friend. Healthy, godly friendships encourage spiritual growth and provide mutual support, while toxic friendships can pull us away from God. Help your teen reflect on their current friendships and how they can nurture godly relationships that honor God and support their faith.

Journaling Questions for Mentor:

1. Reflect on the close friendships in your life. How have your friends influenced your faith and character over the years?

2. What qualities do you think are most important in a godly friendship? How do you see these qualities reflected in your own friendships?

3. Have you ever had to set boundaries in a friendship to protect your relationship with God? How did you handle it, and what was the outcome?

4. How can you encourage your teen to build healthy friendships, and what advice can you offer from your own experience?

5. In what ways can you be a better friend to the people in your life, showing them God's love and support through your words and actions?

Real-Life Story:

William Wilberforce and John Newton: Friendship That Endured Adversity

One famous Christian whose life was profoundly impacted by a friend's encouragement is William Wilberforce, the British politician and social reformer known for his tireless efforts to abolish the slave trade in England. His journey toward faith and perseverance in the face of immense difficulty was greatly influenced by his close friendship with John Newton, the former slave ship captain who became a prominent pastor and abolitionist.

Wilberforce experienced a spiritual awakening in the late 1770s, a time when he was grappling with his purpose in life and the moral implications of his political career. During this period, he sought guidance and support from Newton, who had once been involved in the slave trade himself but later found redemption through faith in Christ. Newton became a mentor and friend to Wilberforce, encouraging him to deepen his relationship with God and to consider the moral implications of his actions in the political sphere. Despite facing significant opposition and ridicule from those who profited from the slave trade, Wilberforce remained committed to the cause of abolition. Newton's wisdom and encouragement provided him with the spiritual fortitude to persevere through the challenges he encountered. Newton often reminded Wilberforce of the importance of faith and obedience to God's calling, emphasizing that true Christians are called to stand up against injustice.

Throughout the years, Wilberforce's resolve grew stronger, and he tirelessly campaigned for the abolition of slavery, introducing bills in Parliament and rallying public support. His faith and commitment were unwavering, fueled by the encouragement and friendship of John Newton. In 1807, after years of struggle, the British Parliament finally passed the Abolition of the Slave Trade Act. Wilberforce's legacy as a champion for justice and human rights is a testament to the impact that a faithful friend can have on one's life. His story demonstrates how encouragement, accountability, and the sharing of faith can lead to transformative action, even in the face of daunting obstacles (Metaxas, 2007).

Discussion or Activity with Teen:

Activity:

Allow your teen to invite a few friends to meet with you this week. Plan something fun to encourage bonding, but also take time to talk about Godly friendships. Play games like Two Truths and a Lie and Would You Rather. Ask them questions that force them to become a little more open. There are many resources online for conversation starters that help you go deeper, but here are a few examples:

1. Given the choice of anyone in the world, whom would you want as a dinner guest? Why?

2. Would you like to be famous? In what way?

3. Before making a phone call, do you ever rehearse what you're going to say? Why?

4. What would constitute a perfect day for you?

5. When did you last sing to yourself? To someone else?

6. If you were able to live to the age of 90 and retain either the mind or body of a 30-year-old for the last 60 years of your life, which would you choose?

7. For what in your life do you feel most grateful?

8. If you could change anything about the way you were raised, what would it be?

9. If you could wake up tomorrow having gained one quality or ability, what would it be?

10. Is there something that you've dreamed of doing for a long time? Why haven't you done it?

or

"Friendship Inventory"

1. Identify Friends: Have your teen make a list of their close friends and people they spend a lot of time with.

2. Evaluate the Impact: Ask them to write a few qualities for each friend — both positive and negative — and reflect on how each friend influences their faith, choices, and attitude. For each friend, they can ask themselves:

   ○ Does this friend encourage my faith or help me make good choices?

   ○ Do I feel supported and uplifted in their presence?

3. Set Friendship Goals: Have them write down one goal for improving each friendship. For example, "encourage my friend when they're feeling down" or "spend less time with friends who encourage negative behavior."

Debrief: Talk about how godly friendships should bring them closer to God and support their growth. Encourage them to focus on friendships that bring out the best in both their faith and character.

Conversation Starter:

"The Power of Positive Influence"

Share some things you have learned about friendship. Use these questions to guide a conversation on how friendships shape our lives:

• "What do you think makes a friendship truly 'godly'?"

- "How do your close friends influence your decisions or your attitude? Are there ways you'd like to improve in choosing or being a friend?"

- "What's one quality you most value in a friend, and how do you see that quality helping you grow closer to God?"

This conversation will help your teen see the importance of surrounding themselves with friends who inspire them to live out their faith and make wise choices.

WEEK 38

BUILDING HEALTHY FRIENDSHIPS

Introduction:

This week, your teen will focus on building healthy friendships, learning about open communication, supporting each other through highs and lows, encouraging spiritual growth, setting boundaries, and prioritizing time with important friends. As a mentor, you can help them see the value of godly friendships and guide them toward developing relationships that reflect God's love and care. Encourage your teen to evaluate their current friendships and think about how they can nurture relationships that build them up in faith.

Practical Challenge:

Teen Challenge: Plan to spend intentional time with a friend this week. Whether it's meeting up to play disc golf, going for a hike, or praying together, make time to connect, share, and grow in your friendship.

Mentor Challenge: This week, intentionally spend time with a friend who has had a positive influence on your life. Whether it's grabbing coffee, going for a walk, or praying together, make time to connect, share, and encourage each other. Talk with your teen about the importance of prioritizing godly friendships and finding time to nurture those relationships.

Bible Story: Jonathan's Encouragement of David (1 Samuel 23:15-18)

Reflection: David was on the run from King Saul, fearing for his life and feeling alone. But in one of his most difficult times, Jonathan, his close friend, came to strengthen his faith and remind him of God's promises. Jonathan sought David out in the wilderness, encouraging him not to be afraid because God would protect him and fulfill His purpose. Jonathan's friendship was a source of hope and courage for David, even when circumstances were overwhelming.

True friendships, like Jonathan and David's, are built on love, trust, and encouragement. They help us through difficult times, reminding us of God's faithfulness and strengthening our faith. This story shows us that godly friends don't just support us emotionally — they point us back to God when we need it most.

Key Themes:

- Godly friendships provide support and encouragement in difficult times.

- Friends who point us back to God help strengthen our faith.

- Real friendship involves showing up when it matters and offering words of hope.

Teen Devotional Recap:

- **Day 1:** *Communicating Openly and Honestly with Friends* – Ephesians 4:24-25 – Open and honest communication builds trust and depth in friendships. Speaking the truth in love helps nurture healthy relationships that are built on understanding and care.

- **Day 2:** *Supporting Each Other Through Good and Bad Times* – Galatians 6:2 – Good friends are there for one another in all circumstances. Sharing each other's burdens and joys deepens your friendship and reflects God's love and support.

- **Day 3:** *Encouraging Spiritual Growth in Your Friendships* – 1 Thessalonians 5:11 – True friends help each other grow spiritually by encouraging one another, praying together, and reminding each other of God's promises.

- **Day 4:** *Setting Boundaries in Friendships* – Proverbs 25:17 – Healthy friendships require boundaries. Respecting each other's time and space is crucial for maintaining balanced relationships.

- **Day 5:** *Making Time for Important Friendships* – John 15:12-13 – Friendships require effort and time. Nurturing the relationships that matter most helps you grow closer and strengthens your bond.

Weekly Summary:

This week, your teen learned about building healthy friendships through open communication, support during difficult times, spiritual encouragement, setting boundaries, and making time for important relationships. Godly friendships require intentionality and care, and when nurtured, they can bring great joy and strength to our lives. Encourage your teen to reflect on their friendships and consider how they can invest more in relationships that point them toward God.

Journaling Questions for Mentor:

1. Reflect on the close friendships in your life. How do open communication and support play a role in keeping those friendships healthy?

2. How can you encourage spiritual growth in your friendships? What steps can you take to make your friendships more centered on God?

3. Think about any friendships in your life where boundaries might need to be set. How can you approach that conversation in a loving and respectful way?

4. Are there friendships that have had a significant impact on your faith? How can you nurture and invest more in those relationships?

5. How can you guide the teen in understanding the importance of building friendships that honor God and support their spiritual growth?

Real-Life Story:

William Carey and Andrew Fuller: The Power of Godly Friendships

William Carey was a British shoemaker and a keen botanist who felt a calling to share the gospel in India. However, his journey was not easy, and it was the encouragement and support of his friend, Andrew Fuller, that helped sustain him during difficult times.

In the late 18th century, Carey faced skepticism and resistance from his contemporaries in England when he first proposed the idea of overseas missionary work. Many doubted the feasibility of his plans and the importance of reaching distant lands. Despite this,

Carey persevered, driven by his deep faith and conviction. During this challenging period, Andrew Fuller became a significant source of encouragement for Carey. Fuller, a Baptist pastor and theologian, believed in Carey's vision and saw the importance of missions. He supported Carey both spiritually and practically, even helping to establish the Baptist Missionary Society in 1792, which sent Carey to India and financially supported him.

When Carey arrived in India in 1793, he faced numerous obstacles, including cultural differences, language barriers, and personal hardships. His early years were marked by struggle, including the death of his wife, Dorothy, and the challenges of establishing a mission in a foreign land. Throughout these trials, Carey often turned to Fuller for encouragement and guidance. Fuller's unwavering belief in Carey's mission helped bolster his spirits during these dark times. Carey's faith and perseverance ultimately led to remarkable achievements in India, including the translation of the Bible into several Indian languages and the establishment of educational institutions. His work laid the foundation for future missionary efforts and demonstrated the power of faith, obedience, and the support of friends in overcoming adversity. William Carey's relationship with Andrew Fuller exemplifies how encouragement and friendship can profoundly impact one's faith journey, especially during times of difficulty and doubt (Piper, 2016).

Discussion or Activity with Teen:

Activity:

Set a date and invite your teen's friends from last week's activity to go to a climbing gym together. If neither you or any of the friends have experience, ask the gym to have someone teach you all how to "belay". After the activity, use the visual of trusting your friend to "belay" to discuss the spiritual implications of being able to trust your friends with more important things in life and have them discuss what that should look like. This encourages a healthy form of social activity while encouraging them spiritually at the same time.

or

"Friendship Goals and Actions"

1. **List Current Friendships**: Have your teen write down the names of close friends with whom they want to build deeper, healthier connections.

2. **Set a Friendship Goal**: For each friend, ask them to set a specific goal that reflects something they'd like to invest in the relationship. Examples could be:

   ◦ "Encourage them through their challenges."

- ○ "Pray together or talk about faith."

- ○ "Spend quality time together, focusing on listening."

3. **Plan Practical Actions**: For each goal, help your teen think of one or two practical steps they can take in the coming week to support their goal. These could include texting the friend an encouraging message, organizing a get-together, or offering a listening ear.

Debrief: Talk about how these small, intentional actions can strengthen godly friendships and create lasting support and joy.

Conversation Starter:

"Investing in Friendships that Matter"

After sharing any additional secrets to success you have learned about friendship, use these questions to guide a conversation on the value of building healthy friendships:

- "What habits or expectations do you think are essential in a friendship that helps you grow closer to God?"

- "What are some ways you can invest more in friendships that mean a lot to you?"

- "Can you think of a time when a friend encouraged you in a tough season? How did that impact your faith?"

This discussion can help your teen reflect on ways to foster relationships that truly nurture their growth and bring joy into their life.

Week 39

Peer Pressure

Introduction:

This week, your teen will focus on recognizing and overcoming peer pressure. They will explore ways to stand up for their beliefs, resist negative influences, and surround themselves with friends who support their faith. As a mentor, you can help your teen develop strategies for standing firm in their values and encourage them to become a leader in their friend group, rather than simply following the crowd. Use this week to discuss how you've dealt with peer pressure in your own life and how God has helped you stay true to your beliefs.

Practical Challenge:

Teen Challenge: This week, identify an area of your life where you face peer pressure and practice saying "no." Whether it's pressure to talk a certain way, act in a way that doesn't reflect your faith, or compromise your values, stand firm and choose God's way over the world's way.

Mentor Challenge: This week, think of a situation in your own life where you face peer pressure. Whether it's pressure at work, within a social group, or in another area of life, practice saying "no" to anything that goes against your faith or values. If you don't have a current situation, share one from the past. Have an open conversation with your teen about how you both can stand firm in the face of peer pressure and encourage each other to make decisions that honor God.

Bible Story: Daniel's Friends Refuse to Bow (Daniel 3)

Reflection: In Daniel 3, Shadrach, Meshach, and Abed-Nego faced incredible peer pressure when King Nebuchadnezzar commanded everyone to bow down to a golden statue. Refusing to compromise their faith in God, the three friends stood firm, knowing the consequences could be severe — even death in a fiery furnace. But their faith didn't waver, and they boldly declared that God could deliver them, but even if He didn't, they wouldn't bow to the statue. In the end, God miraculously saved them from the flames, and their faith became a testimony to the king and the entire kingdom.

This story reminds us that standing up for what we believe in, even under intense pressure, honors God. While standing firm may not always lead to miraculous deliverance, it always leads to God being glorified. Courage, conviction, and unwavering faith can inspire others and serve as a powerful witness to the world.

Key Themes:

- Peer pressure often demands compromise, but standing firm in faith brings honor to God.

- God's protection is not always immediate, but He is always with us in the fire.

- True faith trusts in God, no matter the outcome.

Teen Devotional Recap:

- **Day 1:** *Recognizing the Different Forms of Peer Pressure* – Proverbs 1:10 – Peer pressure can be direct or subtle, and recognizing its presence is the first step in resisting it.

- **Day 2:** *The Importance of Standing Up for What You Believe* – 1 Corinthians 16:13 – Standing firm in your faith is essential, even when it's challenging or unpopular.

- **Day 3:** *Strategies for Saying "No" to Negative Influences* – James 4:7 – Learning to say "no" is key in resisting peer pressure. God gives strength and wisdom to help stand firm.

- **Day 4:** *Surrounding Yourself with People Who Support Your Values* – 1 Samuel 14:7 – Friends who encourage your faith make a significant difference. Good friends sharpen one another's character.

- **Day 5:** *How to Lead Others Instead of Following the Crowd* – 1 Peter 4:4-5 – Being a leader means setting a positive example for others and staying true to your beliefs, no matter what the world says.

Weekly Summary:

This week, your teen learned how to recognize peer pressure, stand firm in their beliefs, and say "no" to negative influences. They explored the importance of surrounding themselves with friends who support their values and how to be a leader who influences others instead of following the crowd. Encourage your teen to stay grounded in their faith and remember that God gives them the strength to stand firm, even in the face of pressure.

Journaling Questions for Mentor:

1. Reflect on a time when you faced peer pressure in your life. How did you respond, and what did you learn from that experience?

2. How have you developed the courage to stand up for your faith in situations where others were pressuring you to conform?

3. Think about the influence your friends and community have on your decisions. How do they help you stay strong in your beliefs?

4. As a mentor, how can you encourage your teen to recognize and resist negative peer pressure? What strategies can you share from your own experiences?

5. How can you help your teen become a leader in their friend group, encouraging them to set a positive example for others?

Real-Life Story:

Sadie Robertson Huff: Standing Firm in Faith

A contemporary Christian who has stood firm in their faith amidst significant peer pressure is Sadie Robertson Huff, a well-known speaker, author, and former star of the reality TV show *Duck Dynasty*. During her teenage years, Sadie experienced intense pressure to conform to the expectations of her peers, especially regarding popularity and lifestyle choices. As she gained fame through the reality show, she found herself in situations where she was often faced with choices that conflicted with her Christian values.

One notable moment came during her high school years when Sadie was invited to attend parties and events where drinking and other risky behaviors were common. Many of her friends were engaging in activities that did not align with her beliefs, and she felt the weight of wanting to fit in while also wanting to honor her faith. In the midst of this pressure, Sadie leaned on her Christian upbringing and the teachings of her family. She chose to be open about her faith, sharing her convictions with her friends, which sometimes led to uncomfortable conversations. Instead of compromising her values, she decided to focus on being a positive influence, encouraging her peers to consider the choices they were making.

Sadie often spoke about the importance of surrounding herself with friends who shared her values and supported her faith journey. She made it clear that her identity was rooted in Christ and that she wanted to be a light in the darkness, even if it meant standing alone at times. This commitment resonated with many of her peers, leading some to respect her choices and even ask her for guidance. Her experiences ultimately shaped her into a strong advocate for living authentically as a Christian, encouraging others to embrace their faith without fear of judgment or rejection. Today, Sadie continues to use her platform to inspire young people to stand firm in their beliefs, demonstrating that it is possible to remain true to one's faith despite societal pressures (Huff, 2020).

Discussion or Activity with Teen:

Activity:

Discuss together any areas where your teen seems to struggle with peer pressure, especially if you had a chance to witness even some small things in your interactions with their friends in past weeks. Pick one specific thing (e.g. using foul language, sarcasm, or inappropriate talk about girls) and ask the teen if they will let you be an accountability partner to help them in that issue. Then check in with your teen about that issue on a regular basis. If you do additional activities with your teen's friends, choose something simple, such as putting your hand on their shoulder, to remind them when they are slipping into that habit without embarrassing them in front of their friends.

or

"Role-Playing Resilience"

1. **Identify Common Scenarios**: Ask your teen to think of scenarios where they have felt or might feel peer pressure, such as being encouraged to skip class, join in gossip, or compromise their values.

2. **Practice Responses**: Choose two or three scenarios and role-play responses

together. Encourage your teen to practice saying "no" confidently, offering alternative activities, or calmly explaining their reasons.

3. **Reflect on Values**: After each role-play, take a moment to discuss how their response reflects their values and why standing firm is important.

Debrief: Share how practicing these responses builds confidence for real-life situations. Reinforce that saying "no" to negative influences helps them stay true to themselves and God's guidance.

Conversation Starter:

"Standing Firm Together"

After sharing some of your own struggles with peer pressure, especially in your teenage years, these questions can help open a discussion about peer pressure and standing firm:

- "What situations do you think are the hardest to say 'no' to, and why?"

- "How do you feel after making a choice that aligns with your values, even when it's unpopular?"

- "Who are some friends or mentors that help you stay grounded? How do they support your decisions?"

This conversation will help your teen identify positive influences and consider strategies for handling peer pressure with resilience.

Week 40

How to Be a Leader Among Friends

Introduction:

This week, your teen will learn about leadership among friends, focusing on leading by example, encouraging others, and demonstrating humility. Being a leader isn't about control or being in charge but about serving others, setting a positive example, and knowing when to step back and let others lead. As a mentor, you can help your teen discover their leadership potential and share personal stories of leadership challenges and victories in your life.

Practical Challenge:

Teen Challenge: Identify one area in your life where you can be a leader this week. Whether it's setting a good example, encouraging a friend, or standing up for what's right, step out in faith and lead others with integrity and love.

Mentor Challenge: Identify an area in your own life where you can step out in leadership this week. Whether it's setting a positive example at work, encouraging someone, or leading in a ministry or project, step out with integrity and love. If you do not have something from the present, then share something from the past with your teen. Share with them how you are applying what you've learned, and encourage them to look for ways to lead by example among their peers.

Bible Story: Joshua Takes Leadership (Joshua 1:1-9)

Reflection: After Moses' death, Joshua was chosen by God to lead the Israelites into the Promised Land. Taking on such a significant leadership role wasn't easy, but God assured Joshua that He would be with him every step of the way. God encouraged Joshua to be strong and courageous, promising success as long as Joshua followed His commands and relied on His guidance. Joshua's confidence as a leader came from his faith in God, not from his own abilities.

Joshua's story shows us that true leadership isn't about having all the answers or being perfect — it's about trusting God, leading with integrity, and stepping out in faith. Whether you're leading your friends, family, or community, God's presence and guidance will give you the strength you need to lead well.

Key Themes:

- God calls us to be strong and courageous in leadership.

- Leadership is about serving others, not seeking power or control.

- God's guidance and presence make all the difference in our ability to lead effectively.

Teen Devotional Recap:

- **Day 1:** *Leading by Example with Integrity* – 1 Timothy 4:12 – Leadership is about setting an example in word, conduct, and faith.

- **Day 2:** *Being a Positive Influence Without Being Controlling* – 1 Peter 2:12 – Leadership is about influence, not control, shining your light to point others to God.

- **Day 3:** *Encouraging Your Friends to Make Good Decisions* – Hebrews 3:13 – Leadership means encouraging others in faith and good decision-making.

- **Day 4:** *Building Confidence as a Leader* – Ephesians 6:10 – God calls leaders to be strong and courageous, trusting in His presence.

- **Day 5:** *Knowing When to Follow and When to Lead* – Matthew 20:26-28 – Humility in leadership involves knowing when to lead and when to serve.

Weekly Summary:

This week, your teen learned about leadership in friendships, focusing on leading by example, encouraging others, and knowing when to step back. They explored how leadership is about serving others and making decisions that honor God. Encourage your teen to be confident in their leadership abilities, trusting that God is with them and will guide them in their relationships and actions.

Journaling Questions for Mentor:

1. Reflect on a time when you had to lead by example. How did it impact those around you, and what challenges did you face?

2. How do you balance being a positive influence without coming across as controlling or overbearing in your relationships?

3. How can you encourage the teen to make wise decisions and lead others in their faith journey?

4. Where have you needed to step out in boldness and lead? How did trusting in God's guidance help you through that experience?

5. How can you practice humility in your leadership, knowing when to step back and let others lead or share in decision-making?

Real-Life Story:

Truett Cathy: Leading Through Service

Truett Cathy, the founder of Chick-fil-A, is a successful leader who embodies Jesus' example of servant leadership. Cathy built his business on Christian principles, particularly emphasizing servant leadership—putting others' needs first, demonstrating humility, and valuing employees and customers alike. He believed that serving others with humility wasn't just ethical but essential for effective leadership. Cathy made it a point to treat employees like family, emphasizing work-life balance, respect, and a supportive culture. This approach, deeply inspired by his Christian faith, extended to Chick-fil-A's customer service model, which remains renowned for kindness and courtesy. His faith-based leadership was grounded in the principle that by serving and uplifting others, a leader creates a thriving, loyal team and an enduring legacy (Cathy, 2007).

Discussion or Activity with Teen:

Activity:

Equip your teen with more "deep" questions like the ones from Week 37. Talk about the questions and then ask your teen to commit to asking one good question each day to at least one of their friends. Debrief at the end of the week to see how it went. Which friends appreciated the questions and which friends tried to ignore or laugh at the questions because they were uncomfortable? How did your teen feel in the process? What did your teen learn about themselves and their friends in the process?

or

"Leading by Example Challenge"

1. **Identify Leadership Actions**: Together, brainstorm a few specific actions that reflect godly leadership in friendships. Examples could include offering encouragement, initiating a prayer together, or helping a friend in need.

2. **Choose an Action Each Day**: Encourage your teen to choose one of these leadership actions to do each day this week. The actions should reflect serving others and showing kindness, helping them lead by example.

3. **Reflect and Journal**: At the end of each day, have your teen jot down a few sentences about their experience. What was the outcome? How did they feel about taking the lead?

Debrief: Discuss how small acts of leadership in friendships can impact others and strengthen relationships. Emphasize that godly leadership is often about small, consistent actions that uplift others.

Conversation Starter:

"Finding Strength in Leadership"

After sharing some of your own experience in the topic, use these questions to discuss their experiences and feelings about being a leader among friends:

- "What qualities do you admire in leaders you look up to, and how can you bring those qualities into your friendships?"

- "Are there moments when you feel unsure about leading? How do you think you could overcome those feelings?"

- "How can we pray for God's guidance and confidence in your role as a friend and leader?"

This conversation can encourage them to see leadership as a journey of serving others with God's help and trusting Him to guide their actions.

WEEK 41

CONFLICT RESOLUTION

Introduction:

This week, your teen will explore how to handle conflict in a godly way, focusing on principles such as approaching others with love, listening well, seeking peaceful resolutions, and being willing to apologize or forgive. Conflict is a normal part of relationships, but learning to resolve it with grace and humility reflects Christ's love. As a mentor, you can share your own experiences in handling conflict and help your teen grow in their understanding of biblical conflict resolution.

Practical Challenge:

Teen Challenge: Choose one conflict in your life that needs resolution. Pray for God's wisdom and guidance, then take steps to approach the person involved, listen well, and seek a peaceful resolution. Be willing to apologize or forgive as needed.

Mentor Challenge: Identify a conflict in your own life that needs resolution. Pray for wisdom and guidance, then approach the person involved with love, seeking a peaceful solution. Share your experience with your teen and encourage them to do the same. Discuss what you both learned about resolving conflict in a godly way.

Bible Story: Abraham and Lot Resolve Conflict (Genesis 13:1-12)

Reflection: Abraham and Lot faced a conflict when their herdsmen began quarreling over land and resources. Instead of allowing the situation to escalate, Abraham took the initiative to resolve the conflict peacefully. He allowed Lot to choose the best land, showing humility and prioritizing peace over his own personal gain. Abraham's willingness to give up something valuable for the sake of harmony demonstrates how important it is to seek peace in relationships.

This story teaches us that sometimes resolving conflict requires us to humble ourselves and prioritize the relationship over being right or getting what we want. By putting the other person's needs first, as Abraham did with Lot, we can maintain unity and reflect God's love in our interactions.

Key Themes:

- Conflict resolution often requires humility and selflessness.

- Prioritizing peace over personal gain strengthens relationships.

- Approaching conflict with a spirit of reconciliation brings lasting harmony.

Teen Devotional Recap:

- **Day 1:** *How to Approach Someone When You're Upset* – Matthew 18:15 – Jesus teaches us to approach conflict with love and directness, speaking calmly and honestly.

- **Day 2:** *The Importance of Listening During Conflict* – James 1:19 – Listening well helps reduce misunderstandings and shows care for the other person's perspective.

- **Day 3:** *Seeking Peaceful Resolutions Based on Love and Respect* – Romans 12:18 – Striving to live peaceably reflects God's heart for unity and harmony in relationships.

- **Day 4:** *When to Apologize and Ask for Forgiveness* – Matthew 5:23-24 – Jesus emphasizes the importance of reconciliation, even before worship, and the healing that comes with asking for forgiveness.

- **Day 5:** *Handling Ongoing Conflict with Grace* – Ephesians 4:2-3 – Ongoing conflicts require patience, humility, and love as we seek to maintain unity.

Weekly Summary:

This week, your teen learned about resolving conflict in a way that honors God. They explored the importance of listening well, approaching others with love and honesty, and seeking peaceful resolutions. Apologizing and asking for forgiveness were also key themes, as well as how to handle ongoing conflicts with grace and patience.

Journaling Questions for Mentor:

1. Reflect on a conflict you've recently experienced. How did you approach it, and what could you have done differently to seek peace?

2. How does listening to others during conflict help you gain better understanding and lead to healthier resolutions?

3. Share a time when you had to apologize or ask for forgiveness. How did it feel, and how did it impact the relationship?

4. In ongoing conflicts, how do you balance the tension between seeking peace and standing firm in your values?

5. What can you do to foster a culture of open communication and peaceful conflict resolution in your family, workplace, or church?

Real-Life Story:

Tony Dungy: Resolving Conflict with Grace

Tony Dungy, a former NFL coach and strong Christian leader, often speaks about resolving conflict with grace and patience. He believes that handling conflicts well is essential not just in sports but in all relationships. Dungy encourages forgiveness and understanding, saying, "You have to treat people the way you want to be treated, and that starts with resolving conflict in a loving way."

One notable example where he practiced this comes from his time as head coach of the Indianapolis Colts when he was asked to confront the approach of his former assistant, Lovie Smith, who coached the Chicago Bears. Some fans and media pushed Dungy to create a rivalry narrative leading up to the Super Bowl XLI face-off in 2007, but Dungy resisted. Instead of framing it as a competition against Smith, he showed respect and highlighted their shared values and faith as Christians. Rather than taking an adversarial stance, he publicly expressed admiration for Smith, and they even prayed together before the game.

Dungy's approach diffused tension and fostered mutual respect, helping both coaches feel they could play with dignity rather than hostility. This was significant because it illustrated how Dungy values relationships and personal integrity over public rivalry. His humility and grace in this situation were widely appreciated, setting a powerful example for players and fans alike. His example reminds us that whether we are on a team, in school, or at home, handling conflict with grace and respect reflects God's love (Dungy, 2008).

Discussion or Activity with Teen:

Activity:

Read the story of Abraham and Lot in Genesis 13:1-12 and discuss how Abraham approached the conflict with humility and a desire for peace. Ask your teen how they would handle a similar situation and what steps they could take to prioritize peace in their relationships. Together, identify any conflicts each of you are currently facing and pray for God's wisdom and grace to resolve them with love and humility. Then take active steps to resolve those conflicts.

or

"Conflict Resolution Role Play"

1. **Choose Common Scenarios**: Together, brainstorm a few realistic scenarios that might lead to conflict among friends or family. Examples could include a misunderstanding over expectations, a disagreement over a shared project, or hurt feelings from a miscommunication.

2. **Role-Play Solutions**: For each scenario, take turns role-playing as each person involved. Practice using kind words, active listening, and calm tones to work through the conflict. Emphasize using "I" statements, like "I feel..." or "I need...," and practice offering sincere apologies.

3. **Reflect on Solutions**: After each role-play, discuss how the approach made each person feel and what worked well in the resolution. Consider what actions showed respect, empathy, and a desire for peace.

Debrief: Encourage your teen to apply what they learned next time a conflict arises. Remind them that even when conflicts are challenging, God values their effort to work toward peace and understanding.

Conversation Starter:

"Growing Through Conflict"

After sharing about your own growth in conflict resolution, use these questions to help them open up about their experiences and thoughts on resolving conflicts:

- "Can you remember a time when a conflict was resolved in a way that brought you and the other person closer?"

- "What do you think makes a good apology, and how does it make a difference in repairing relationships?"

- "How can we pray for God's help to handle conflicts with patience and grace?"

This conversation will help your teen understand that conflicts can be opportunities for growth and that God's wisdom can guide them toward peace.

Week 42

Forgiveness

Introduction:

Forgiveness is a foundational part of the Christian faith, but it's often one of the hardest principles to live out. This week, as you walk alongside your teen, encourage them to explore forgiveness as a journey toward freedom. Share openly about how forgiveness has impacted your life, perhaps including times when forgiving or seeking forgiveness led to peace and healing.

Practical Challenge:

Teen Challenge: Identify one person you need to forgive this week. Pray for the strength to forgive them, ask God to help you let go of any bitterness, and take a step toward releasing that person from the debt they owe you. Trust God to bring healing and freedom as you forgive.

Mentor Challenge: Join your teen in this week's practical challenge by considering someone you need to forgive. Pray for the strength to release any bitterness and ask God to help you forgive from your heart. Share this experience with your teen as a way to encourage them in their own journey toward forgiveness.

Bible Story: The Parable of the Unforgiving Servant (Matthew 18:21-35)

Reflection: In this parable, Jesus illustrates the importance of forgiveness by comparing a servant who was forgiven an enormous debt yet refuses to forgive a small debt owed to him by someone else. The parable highlights that, because God has forgiven us so completely, we are called to extend that forgiveness to others. God's forgiveness is the foundation of our faith and our example for how to forgive others.

Key Themes:

- Extravagant Forgiveness from God: God forgives us of a debt we could never repay. This example of boundless forgiveness shows us how we are called to forgive others.

- The Danger of Holding onto Unforgiveness: The unforgiving servant is ultimately punished because of his refusal to forgive. This illustrates how unforgiveness can harm us and our relationships with others.

- Forgiveness as an Act of Freedom: By forgiving others, we are freeing ourselves from the bondage of bitterness and opening the door to healing and reconciliation.

Teen Devotional Recap:

- **Day 1:** *Understanding What Forgiveness Really Means* – Matthew 18:21-22 – Forgiveness is a choice to release bitterness and to leave justice in God's hands.

- **Day 2:** *How Unforgiveness Hurts You More Than Others* – Hebrews 12:15 – Unforgiveness can poison our hearts, spreading bitterness and affecting our mental, emotional, and spiritual well-being.

- **Day 3:** *Offering Forgiveness Even When It's Hard* – Matthew 6:14 – Jesus teaches us that offering forgiveness is essential to living in His grace, even when it's difficult.

- **Day 4:** *The Connection Between God's Forgiveness and Ours* – Colossians 3:13 – Reflecting on God's forgiveness for us helps us to forgive others with compassion and grace.

- **Day 5:** *Learning to Forgive Yourself* – 2 Corinthians 5:17 – Accepting God's forgiveness means letting go of self-condemnation and embracing new life in Christ.

Weekly Summary:

This week, we focused on the meaning of forgiveness, how unforgiveness harms us, the strength to forgive when it's hard, understanding God's forgiveness as the basis of ours, and learning to forgive ourselves. Forgiveness is a powerful path to freedom and healing, allowing us to live fully in God's grace.

Journaling Questions for Mentor:

1. Think of a time when you struggled with forgiving someone. How did God help you through the process?

2. How has unforgiveness impacted your relationships, faith, or sense of peace in the past?

3. What's a moment when you experienced God's forgiveness in a life-changing way, and how did it shape your ability to forgive others?

4. How can you help your teen or others understand the connection between receiving God's forgiveness and forgiving themselves?

5. Is there someone you still need to forgive? What steps can you take toward releasing that bitterness?

Real-Life Story:

Corrie ten Boom: The Power of Forgiveness

Corrie ten Boom, a Dutch Christian who helped many Jews escape the Nazis during World War II, was arrested and sent to Ravensbrück concentration camp for her efforts. After the war, Corrie dedicated her life to sharing her experiences and the message of forgiveness and healing that she had found in her faith. One of the most poignant moments in her life occurred when she encountered one of the guards from Ravensbrück. This guard had been particularly brutal, and Corrie had experienced great suffering at his hands. Years after the war, while speaking at a church in Munich, she was surprised to see the former guard approach her after her talk.

As he came forward, Corrie recognized him instantly, and a wave of emotions rushed over her. He introduced himself and said, "I have done terrible things, but I have come to ask for your forgiveness." He explained that he had since become a Christian and realized the depths of his wrongdoing. In that moment, Corrie felt a deep conflict within her. Her heart was torn between the pain of her past and the message of forgiveness that she had preached. The memories of the suffering and the loss of her family in the concentration camp flooded back to her. However, she knew that forgiveness was essential for her own healing and that of others.

She prayed for strength, and as she looked at the man before her, she extended her hand to him. She later described the act of reaching out as something she felt she couldn't do on her own; it was only through God's grace that she could offer forgiveness. As their hands touched, Corrie felt an overwhelming sense of love and forgiveness wash over her, both for him and for herself. In that powerful moment, she realized that forgiveness is not just a feeling but an act of the will—a choice to let go of the past and embrace the possibility of healing. This encounter reinforced her belief that God's love transcends all, even the deepest wounds caused by human cruelty (Ten Boom, 2006).

Corrie ten Boom's story illustrates the incredible power of forgiveness, even in the face of unimaginable suffering, and her life continues to inspire many to seek reconciliation and healing in their own lives. She later said, "Forgiveness is the key that unlocks the door of resentment and the handcuffs of hatred. It is a power that breaks the chains of bitterness and the shackles of selfishness" (Ten Boom, 1982). Corrie's life teaches us that forgiveness, even in the face of deep hurt, is possible through God's grace.

Discussion or Activity with Teen:

Activity:

Help your teen reflect on whether there is anyone in their life that they need to offer forgiveness to. If there is an issue of forgiveness that can be dealt with in person, offer to join them and support them in having that conversation or allow them to role play with you until they have the confidence to do it themselves. If there is someone in your life that you need to offer forgiveness to, set the example for your teen and make a point to have that conversation this week.

or

"Forgiveness Letter"

1. **Reflect on Past Hurts**: Encourage your teen to think of a person they need to forgive or an area where they struggle to forgive themselves. You do the same.

2. **Write a Letter**: Each of you then write a letter expressing your feelings about what happened. If it involves forgiving someone else, write down the hurt you experienced, but also write down your decision to release that hurt and forgive. If it's about forgiving yourself, you can write about the reasons you feel guilty or regretful and why you need to forgive yourself. Acknowledge in your letters that Jesus' sacrifice is sufficient to cover *every* sin.

3. **Symbolic Release**: When you are both ready, safely destroy your letters,

whether by tearing them up, burning them, or tossing them away. This physical act symbolizes letting go of the burden of unforgiveness and leaving it with God.

4. **Prayer for Healing**: Close with a prayer together, asking God for healing, strength, and freedom from any lingering resentment or shame.

Debrief: Emphasize that forgiveness doesn't mean what happened was okay but forgiveness is a step toward peace and healing. Remind your teen that God is always ready to help them release these burdens.

Conversation Starter:

"Experiencing God's Forgiveness and Sharing It with Others"

Share with your teen a story of a time when forgiveness brought you healing. Encourage them to think about how letting go of bitterness and forgiving others opens them up to God's peace and freedom. You could also discuss how holding onto unforgiveness affects relationships, both with others and with God. After sharing your own story about forgiveness, use these questions to help your teen think about the significance of forgiveness in their life:

- "When have you felt God's forgiveness in a powerful way? How did it make you feel?"

- "Is there someone in your life whom you need to forgive, or maybe an area where you need to forgive yourself?"

- "How can you ask God for the strength to forgive, even when it's hard?"

These questions will help your teen reflect on the freedom forgiveness brings and encourage them to rely on God's grace in all aspects of their journey toward healing.

WEEK 43

SERVING OTHERS

Introduction:

Serving others is an essential part of a Christ-centered life. This week, as you encourage your teen to embrace a heart of service, be prepared to share stories of how service has impacted your own life. Your experiences and wisdom can inspire them to see serving others as a powerful way to reflect Christ's love.

Practical Challenge:

Teen Challenge: Choose one person or place to serve this week. Whether it's a family member, friend, neighbor, or community organization, look for an opportunity to serve without expecting anything in return. Ask God to use your service to show His love to others.

Mentor Challenge: Participate in the practical challenge alongside your teen this week. Look for a specific person or place to serve and intentionally give of yourself without expecting anything in return. Afterward, share the experience with your teen, emphasizing how service brought you closer to God and helped you reflect His love. This is a great time to do something together with your teen, if possible. (See the Activity for the end of the week.)

Bible Story: Jesus Washes the Disciples' Feet (John 13:1-17)

Reflection: In this passage, Jesus, the Son of God, takes on the role of a servant by washing His disciples' feet. In doing so, He models humility, compassion, and selflessness. Washing feet was typically a task for the lowest servant, yet Jesus willingly served His disciples in this way to teach them the importance of serving one another. He reminds us that following Him means embodying humility and loving others through our actions.

Key Themes:

- Humility in Service: Jesus shows us that true greatness comes from humility and serving others.

- Love in Action: Service is a way to put love into practice. Jesus' act of washing feet was a tangible way of showing His love for His disciples.

- Invitation to Serve: Jesus calls His followers to serve others with the same love and humility He demonstrated. When we serve others, we are following in His footsteps and honoring His example.

Teen Devotional Recap:

- **Day 1:** *Why Serving Others is Part of Following Jesus* – Philippians 2:5-8 – Jesus set the ultimate example of humble service, and we are called to follow His lead.

- **Day 2:** *Small Ways to Serve Those Around You Daily* – Galatians 5:13 – Even small acts of service done with love can make a big impact.

- **Day 3:** *Serving with a Humble Heart, Without Expecting Anything in Return* – Acts 20:35 – True service seeks to give, not to receive, mirroring Jesus' selfless love.

- **Day 4:** *How Service Helps You Grow Closer to God* – Matthew 25:40 – Serving others deepens our relationship with God and aligns us with His heart.

- **Day 5:** *The Impact of Serving in Your Community* – Romans 12:6-8 – Using our gifts to serve others allows us to contribute to God's work and make an impact in our community.

Weekly Summary:

This week, we focused on serving others as a core aspect of following Jesus. Serving others, whether through small acts of kindness or larger commitments, allows us to reflect Christ's love, grow in humility, and deepen our connection with God. Each act of service, no matter how small, is an opportunity to show God's love and make a difference in the lives of those around us.

Journaling Questions for Mentor:

1. Think of a time when you served someone without expecting anything in return. How did it impact you and your relationship with God?

2. What are some of the small, everyday ways you can model a heart of service to your teen or those around you?

3. Reflect on a time when someone served you with humility. How did it influence your perspective on serving others?

4. In what ways has serving others helped you grow closer to God?

5. How can you encourage your teen to serve using their unique gifts and talents?

Real-Life Story:

Mother Teresa: A Life of Selfless Service

Mother Teresa dedicated her life to serving the poorest of the poor in India. One powerful story of Mother Teresa's compassion involves a man she found lying in a Calcutta gutter, extremely ill and covered in sores. Many people had walked by him, dismissing him as just another beggar, but she saw his suffering and decided to care for him herself. She took him to her home for the dying, where she washed and cleaned his wounds, fed him, and stayed by his side. Despite his pain, he felt love and dignity for the first time in years. In his final moments, he told her, "I have lived like an animal in the streets, but I am going to die like an angel, loved and cared for" (Nobel Prize Outreach AB 2024, Nov. 2024)

This small but profound act reflects how Mother Teresa saw every person as worthy of love and care. Her unwavering commitment to showing kindness to individuals, one at a time, defined her approach to service. Her selfless acts of love and service touched countless lives and inspired others to serve. Mother Teresa's life reminds us that serving others doesn't have to be complicated — it's about showing love in practical ways and putting others before ourselves.

Discussion or Activity with Teen:

Activity:

Serving Together as Friends or Family

Consider choosing a service activity you and your teen can do together. Whether it's volunteering at a local food bank, helping a neighbor with yard work, or writing encouraging notes to people in your community, serving as a family and with friends can make a lasting impact. Afterward, take time to discuss how serving together made you feel and how it brought you closer to God and each other.

or

"Acts of Kindness Challenge"

1. **Identify Areas to Serve**: Encourage your teen to think of 3–5 small acts of kindness they can do for others this week. These could include simple things like holding the door open, helping with chores, encouraging a friend, or spending time with someone who might be lonely.

2. **Daily Act of Service**: Challenge them to complete one small act of kindness each day. If they're open to it, they can jot down what they did, how it felt, and how the person reacted.

3. **Reflect on the Experience**: At the end of the week, ask your teen to reflect on their experiences and what they learned from serving others.

4. **Prayer of Thanks**: Close with a prayer, thanking God for the opportunities to serve and asking Him to continue opening doors to reflect His love through their actions.

Debrief: Remind your teen that serving isn't about grand gestures but about showing love through everyday actions. Even small acts of kindness can make a big impact on someone's day.

Conversation Starter:

"Learning to Serve with a Heart Like Jesus"

After sharing about how serving has impacted your life, use these questions to guide a conversation about the value of service and how it deepens their faith:

- "What's one act of kindness you did this week that made you feel close to God?"

- "How do you think serving others can help you grow in your relationship with God?"

- "Are there areas of your life where you feel God may be calling you to serve in a deeper way?"

These questions will help your teen see service as a way to connect with God and understand that every act of kindness reflects Christ's love.

WEEK 44

LOVING PEOPLE WHO ARE HARD TO LOVE

Introduction:

Loving difficult people can be one of the greatest challenges of our faith, but it's also an area where we can grow deeply in Christ's character. As you journey through this week with your teen, encourage them to see challenging relationships as an opportunity for spiritual growth and a chance to reflect God's love. By modeling forgiveness, setting healthy boundaries, and praying for those who are hard to love, you can help them embrace this Christ-like approach to relationships.

Practical Challenge:

Teen Challenge: Choose one person who has been difficult for you to love and begin praying for them daily. Ask God to soften your heart, help you forgive, and show you practical ways to love them with God's love. Look for opportunities to show kindness to them throughout the week.

Mentor Challenge: This week, choose one challenging relationship in your own life to pray over. Spend time asking God for strength to forgive, set healthy boundaries if needed, and actively show kindness in a way that reflects His love. Share this experience with your teen, showing them how God is working in you to extend love even in tough situations. Your vulnerability will encourage your teen to recognize we are all in process and that God is like a gardner working on each of us to help us produce more fruit.

Bible Story: The Good Samaritan (Luke 10:25-37)

Reflection: In this parable, Jesus shares the story of a Samaritan man who stops to help a wounded Jewish man. Despite the historical and cultural tensions between Jews and Samaritans, this man chooses compassion over prejudice, crossing social boundaries to show kindness and mercy. The Good Samaritan serves as a powerful example of loving those who may be considered "enemies" or hard to love, teaching us that genuine love and compassion transcend differences and hostility.

Key Themes:

- Compassion Over Judgment: True love shows compassion without discrimination. The Samaritan's choice to help demonstrates God's love, which sees past hostility and conflict.

- Sacrificial Service: The Samaritan didn't just acknowledge the man's need; he went out of his way to help, despite the cost. Loving those who are hard to love often requires sacrifice.

- Living Out God's Love: Jesus calls us to "go and do likewise," encouraging us to love others, even those who may be challenging to love, in a way that reflects God's heart.

Teen Devotional Recap:

- **Day 1:** *God's Command to Love Your Enemies* – Matthew 5:44 – Jesus challenges us to love those who are difficult to love, mirroring God's unconditional love for us.

- **Day 2:** *Practical Ways to Show Love to Difficult People* – Romans 12:20 – Loving others sometimes means showing kindness in unexpected ways, even when it feels hard.

- **Day 3:** *Setting Boundaries While Still Loving Others* – 2 Timothy 3:2-5 – Loving people doesn't mean tolerating harmful behavior; boundaries can help us love from a place of strength.

- **Day 4:** *Praying for Those Who Hurt or Mistreat You* – Luke 6:28 – Praying for those who hurt us can heal our hearts and help us see them through God's eyes.

- **Day 5:** *How Loving Difficult People Changes Your Heart* – 1 John 4:7 – Loving difficult people transforms us, growing our compassion and helping us become more like Christ.

Weekly Summary:

This week, we focused on God's call to love those who are hard to love. We explored practical ways to show kindness, the importance of setting boundaries, the healing power of prayer, and the transformative nature of loving those who may be challenging to love. Loving others, especially those who are difficult, is a journey that draws us closer to God's heart and helps us grow in Christ-like love.

Journaling Questions for Mentor:

1. Think of a person who has been hard to love. What has God taught you through that relationship, and how can you share that lesson with your teen?

2. How has praying for someone who has hurt you changed your heart or perspective toward them?

3. In what ways has setting boundaries helped you love others more effectively without compromising your own well-being?

4. Reflect on a time when someone showed you grace or kindness, even if you may not have deserved it. How did that experience impact you?

5. How can you encourage your teen to see difficult relationships as opportunities for growth, rather than obstacles?

Real-Life Story:

Dr. Martin Luther King Jr.: Loving Your Enemies

Dr. Martin Luther King Jr. led a movement of non-violence and love in the face of racism and hatred. He preached about loving your enemies and famously said, "Love is the only force capable of transforming an enemy into a friend" (King, 2012). One of the most famous examples of Martin Luther King Jr. showing love to an "enemy" happened in 1960, during a book signing in Harlem. A woman named Izola Curry approached him, asked if he was really Martin Luther King Jr., and when he confirmed, she plunged a letter opener into his chest. The blade was lodged dangerously close to his aorta, and doctors said any sudden movement could have killed him.

King underwent surgery and survived. Despite the attack, he publicly expressed no anger toward Curry. Instead, he later reflected on the incident, showing compassion and empathy for her troubled state of mind. He acknowledged the difficulties faced by those who harbor such hatred and spoke of his desire for people to respond with understanding and love, even in the face of violence. King's response showed his deep commitment to nonviolence and the transformative power of love and forgiveness, even toward someone who had intended to take his life. Despite facing persecution, he chose to respond with love and grace, showing the power of God's love to change hearts and bring about peace. Dr. King's life teaches us that loving difficult people is not just about being nice — it's a powerful way to bring God's love and transformation to the world (*Curry, Izola Ware,* The Martin Luther King, Jr. Research and Education Institute).

Discussion or Activity with Teen:

Activity:

Identify and Pray Together for a Difficult Relationship

Sit down with your teen and encourage them to share about a relationship in their life that has been challenging. Together, spend time praying over this relationship, asking God to give both of you compassion, patience, and the strength to love as He does. Encourage your teen to let go of any bitterness and focus on forgiveness.

or

"Prayer and Kindness Journal"

1. **Identify One Difficult Person**: Ask your teen to think of one person in their life they find challenging to love. This could be someone at school, in their family, or in their friend group.

2. **Daily Prayer**: Encourage your teen to pray specifically for this person each day. They can ask God for strength, patience, and guidance on how to show love, as well as for any needs this person may have.

3. **Acts of Kindness**: Each day, encourage your teen to do one small act of kindness for this person if possible — it could be as simple as offering a smile, a compliment, or assistance when needed.

4. **Reflection Journal**: Have them jot down any changes they notice in themselves or in their feelings toward this person. This could include how their heart may soften, any growth in patience, or a greater sense of peace about the situation.

5. **Prayer of Thanks**: At the end of the week, close with a prayer, thanking God for the opportunity to learn to love more deeply and asking for continued growth in love and patience.

Debrief: Remind your teen that sometimes, loving others changes us more than it changes them. God can use these experiences to refine our character and help us see others through His eyes.

Conversation Starter:

"Learning to Love Difficult People with God's Help"

Talk to your teen about how you've handled difficult relationships in your own life. Share the ways God has guided you, especially in setting boundaries, praying for the other person, and learning to forgive. Encourage them to see these relationships as part of their faith journey, reminding them that God is with them every step of the way. Use these questions to guide a conversation about the challenge and growth of loving those who are hard to love:

- "What was it like to pray for and show kindness to someone you find challenging to love?"

- "How do you think God is working in your heart through this experience?"

- "What are some qualities you admire about Jesus' love, especially for those who were difficult to love? How can you reflect those qualities in your own life?"

These questions will help your teen reflect on the spiritual growth that comes from loving others, even when it's challenging, and see it as an opportunity to grow closer to God.

WEEK 45

BEING KIND IN A HARSH WORLD

Introduction:

Kindness is one of the simplest yet most powerful ways to reflect God's love. In today's world, where harshness and judgment are often the norm, small acts of kindness can make a lasting difference. As you go through this week with your teen, emphasize that kindness is not merely an action but a reflection of Christ's love in us. Encourage them to look for opportunities to choose kindness, even in challenging situations, and to see each act as a way to show God's love to others.

Practical Challenge:

Teen Challenge: Look for one opportunity each day this week to show kindness to someone, especially those who may not expect it. Whether it's through encouraging words, helping someone with a need, paying it forward, or simply being a good listener, choose to reflect God's love through your actions.

Mentor Challenge: This week, focus on showing kindness to someone who may not expect it. Whether it's through a word of encouragement, helping someone in need, or simply being a patient listener, look for opportunities to show God's love through your actions. Share your experience with your teen, discussing how these acts of kindness reflect God's heart.

Bible Story: The Woman Caught in Adultery – John 8:1-11

Reflection: The story of the woman caught in adultery reveals Jesus' compassion, kindness, and grace. While the religious leaders were quick to condemn and shame her, Jesus responded with love and understanding. Rather than joining in their harshness, He challenged them to look at their own hearts, saying, "Let any one of you who is without sin be the first to throw a stone at her." When everyone left, Jesus offered the woman forgiveness and a new beginning, telling her, "Go now and leave your life of sin." Jesus' response reminds us that we are called to treat others with kindness and grace, even when they make mistakes or fall short. He saw the woman's value beyond her failures and extended kindness when others offered judgment.

Key Themes:

- Choosing Compassion Over Condemnation: Jesus didn't join the crowd in condemning the woman. Instead, He showed her kindness, reminding us to choose compassion and empathy over judgment.

- Recognizing Our Own Humanity: Jesus' response — "Whoever is without sin, cast the first stone" — asks us to examine our own hearts. None of us is without fault, so we should approach others with humility rather than harshness.

- Offering Forgiveness and Encouragement: Jesus' kindness didn't condone the woman's actions; instead, He offered her a chance to change. He encouraged her to leave her life of sin and walk in a new direction, showing that kindness can inspire transformation and healing.

Teen Devotional Recap:

- **Day 1:** *Why Kindness Matters More Than Ever* – Ephesians 4:32 – Kindness is a powerful way to show God's love in a world that can often be unkind.

- **Day 2:** *The Ripple Effect of Small Acts of Kindness* – Proverbs 16:24 – Small acts of kindness can have a lasting impact, bringing encouragement and healing to others.

- **Day 3:** *Overcoming the Temptation to Be Harsh or Cruel* – Colossians 3:12 – Kindness is a choice, especially in moments when it's easier to be harsh.

- **Day 4:** *Responding with Kindness in Tough Situations* – Luke 6:31 – Responding with kindness, even when others are unkind, reflects God's love.

- **Day 5:** *Kindness as a Reflection of God's Love* – Titus 3:4-5 – God's kindness led to our salvation, and we are called to show His love to others in the same way.

Weekly Summary:

This week, we explored why kindness is essential in a harsh world and how even small acts can make a big difference. We discussed how to overcome the temptation to be harsh, the importance of responding with kindness in tough situations, and how kindness is a powerful reflection of God's love. By choosing kindness, we demonstrate God's compassion and grace in our daily lives.

Journaling Questions for Mentor:

1. Think of a time when someone showed you unexpected kindness. How did it impact you, and how can you pay it forward this week?

2. What situations in your life make it challenging to respond with kindness? How can you rely on God's strength in those moments?

3. Reflect on a time when you had the opportunity to be kind but missed it. What would you do differently if given a second chance?

4. Who in your life could use a little extra kindness right now? How can you show them compassion and love?

5. How does showing kindness help you grow in your relationship with God?

Real-Life Story:

Fred Rogers (Mr. Rogers): Spreading Kindness One Person at a Time

Fred Rogers, known as "Mr. Rogers," was the beloved host of *Mister Rogers' Neighborhood*, a children's television program that focused on kindness, love, and understanding. Fred was known for saying, "There are three ways to ultimate success: The first way is to be kind. The second way is to be kind. The third way is to be kind" (Harris, 2013). Fred Rogers demonstrated his commitment to kindness and compassion in countless ways off-screen. One touching example involved a young boy with cerebral palsy who was a longtime fan of *Mister Rogers' Neighborhood*. The boy's condition made it challenging for him to express his emotions, but his family arranged for him to meet Fred Rogers in person. When Rogers arrived, the boy became so overwhelmed that he started hitting himself out of frustration. Rather than showing discomfort or backing away, Rogers immediately knelt beside the boy, took his hand gently, and began speaking softly to him. Then he asked the boy, "Would you do something for me? Would you pray for me?" The boy was stunned, as he felt he had nothing to offer someone like Fred Rogers, but the request empowered him. Later, Rogers explained to those around him that asking for help can be one of the greatest ways to show love and respect for someone else (Brooks, 2018).

Rogers's sensitivity and his request for the boy's prayers transformed what could have been an awkward encounter into a moment of deep connection, kindness, and dignity. Mr. Rogers demonstrated that small acts of kindness could make a lasting impact on both children and adults alike. His life encourages us to spread kindness, one person at a time, and to live out God's love in our daily interactions.

Discussion or Activity with Teen:

Activity:

Find a person that the two of you can show an act of kindness to together. Maybe an older neighbor does not take care of their yard. Volunteer to clean up the yard together. Find a homeless person and ask them their story. If you have any refugees in your city, volunteer to help them adjust to their new home in America and ask them their story. One of the kindest things you can do is listen to someone's story to help them know they are seen and heard.

or

"Acts of Kindness Challenge"

1. **Daily Kindness Goals**: Encourage your teen to choose one specific act of kindness each day this week. This could be as simple as giving someone a compliment, helping with a chore at home, or reaching out to someone who seems down.

2. **Kindness Jar**: Each time they perform an act of kindness, have them write it down on a slip of paper and place it in a "Kindness Jar." This will give them a visual reminder of how their small acts of kindness add up over the week.

3. **Reflection**: At the end of the week, ask them to read through each slip of paper and reflect on the impact of these small acts. Discuss any changes they noticed in themselves, such as feeling more connected to others or seeing others in a new light.

4. **Prayer of Gratitude**: Close the activity with a prayer of gratitude, asking God

to continue to cultivate kindness in their heart and help them reflect His love in all interactions.

Debrief: Remind your teen that kindness, no matter how small, is powerful. It can bring encouragement, lift someone's day, and reflect God's compassion to others.

Conversation Starter:

"Reflecting God's Love Through Kindness"

Share with your teen a time when kindness changed your perspective or helped you through a difficult time. Discuss why kindness is sometimes difficult, especially when others are rude or unkind. Discuss how it is counter-cultural to sitcoms and memes. Encourage them to choose kindness as a way to be a light in challenging situations. Use these questions to discuss the importance and impact of kindness:

- "What are some ways you've seen kindness make a difference in someone's day?"

- "How does it feel when someone shows kindness to you? How do you think your kindness affects others?"

- "Why do you think God wants us to choose kindness, even when it's difficult? How does it reflect His love?"

These questions will encourage your teen to see kindness as a meaningful, daily choice that reflects God's love and shows compassion to others.

WEEK 46

BUILDING BRIDGES, NOT WALLS

Introduction:

This week, the focus is on cultivating connections with people who may be different from us or those we don't know well. Building bridges is about reaching out with empathy, finding common ground, and breaking down walls of prejudice. As you journey through this week with your teen, encourage them to take steps toward building relationships and understanding, especially with those they may find challenging to connect with. Emphasize that God's love can help us overcome any barriers and build lasting, meaningful connections.

Practical Challenge:

Teen Challenge: Choose one person you don't know very well or someone who is different from you and make an effort to connect with them this week. Look for common ground, listen to their story, and be intentional about building a bridge of understanding and friendship.

Mentor Challenge: Identify a neighbor, colleague, or acquaintance you don't know very well, or someone with a different background. Reach out this week, invite them for coffee, or simply start a conversation to get to know them better. Look for common ground, show genuine interest in their story, and pray for God's love to guide your interaction. Exchange stories with your teen and discuss what you learned in the process.

Bible Story: Jesus and the Samaritan Woman (John 4:1-26)

Reflection: Jesus's interaction with the Samaritan woman at the well is a beautiful example of breaking down social and cultural walls. Samaritans and Jews held deep-seated animosities, yet Jesus didn't let cultural barriers stop Him from reaching out. By engaging the Samaritan woman with compassion and truth, He showed that God's love crosses all boundaries.

Key Themes:

- Crossing Cultural Barriers: Jesus's willingness to speak with a Samaritan woman reflects His desire to reach all people, regardless of social divisions.

- Offering Dignity and Respect: Jesus showed respect to the woman, listening to her story and offering her "living water" for her soul.

- Transforming Lives Through Connection: This simple act of reaching out led the woman to believe in Him, ultimately transforming her life and her community.

Teen Devotional Recap:

- **Day 1:** *The Importance of Empathy and Understanding* – Romans 12:15 – Empathy is the foundation of building bridges; it allows us to connect and understand others deeply.

- **Day 2:** *Finding Common Ground with People Different from You* – 1 Corinthians 9:22 – Finding common ground helps us connect and build bridges across differences.

- **Day 3:** *Overcoming Prejudice and Stereotypes* – James 2:1 – Overcoming prejudice means seeing people as God sees them, without bias or judgment.

- **Day 4:** *Building Meaningful Connections* – Psalm 133:1&3 – Building relationships requires effort, creating a supportive community where people grow together.

- **Day 5:** *The Power of Unity in Christ* – Galatians 3:28 – In Christ, we are united beyond our differences, reflecting God's love and acceptance to the world.

Weekly Summary:

This week, we explored the importance of building bridges and not walls. We discussed empathy, finding common ground, overcoming prejudice, building meaningful connections, and embracing unity in Christ. Building bridges allows us to reflect God's love in a way that unites, strengthens, and brings peace to our relationships.

Journaling Questions for Mentor:

1. Think about someone you may not know well or who is different from you. What are some ways you could reach out and build a connection with them this week?

2. Reflect on a time when you held a stereotype or judgment about someone. How did getting to know them change your perception?

3. How can seeing others through God's eyes help you to overcome prejudices and build bridges in your community?

4. Consider a relationship in your life that needs healing. How might taking steps toward empathy and understanding help to restore it?

5. In what ways can you model unity in Christ within your community, family, or workplace?

Real-Life Story:

William and Catherine Booth: Building Bridges to the Poor

William and Catherine Booth, founders of The Salvation Army, dedicated their lives to building bridges to those who were often ignored — the poor, the addicted, and the homeless. They believed that every person deserved to hear the gospel and be treated with dignity and respect. One powerful story of William and Catherine Booth overcoming prejudice to serve others occurred in the early days of their ministry in London's East End. At the time, the area was riddled with poverty, alcoholism, and crime, and the destitute people living there were often looked down upon by society, even by many churches. One evening, William Booth encountered a man who was lying unconscious in a gutter, drunk and visibly neglected. Many others walked past, dismissing him as a hopeless "drunkard" unworthy of help. However, Booth saw the man's suffering rather than his reputation. He knelt beside him, helped him up, and personally escorted him to a nearby shelter, where he made sure the man was fed, given new clothes, and provided with a place to sleep.

This was no isolated act; Booth and his wife, Catherine, were known for rejecting societal stereotypes and welcoming people society shunned, treating them with dignity and compassion. Their unwavering commitment to seeing value in everyone became a foundational principle of The Salvation Army, which they founded as a movement to break down barriers and bring hope to the marginalized and outcast. By meeting both physical and spiritual needs, the Booths broke down walls of prejudice and showed the love of Christ to those who were hurting (Green, 2006).

Discussion or Activity with Teen:

Activity:

Bridge Builder Bingo

Create a simple "Bridge Builder Bingo" card with acts of kindness or ways to connect with others. Examples could include:

- Start a conversation with someone you don't know well.

- Help someone with a task or project.

- Ask someone about their day and listen fully.

- Invite someone new to join you in an activity.

Throughout the week, encourage your teen to complete as many "Bridge Builder" activities as they can. At the end of the week, reflect on what they learned from reaching out and connecting with others.

or

"Bridge-Building Challenge"

1. **Identify Three People**: Ask your teen to choose three people in their life — a friend, classmate, family member, or even someone they don't know very well — with whom they could build a stronger connection. Encourage them to focus especially on someone who may have a different background or perspective than they do.

2. **Connect through Empathy**: For each person, challenge your teen to find a

way to connect with them this week. This could be through asking about their interests, offering help, listening to their story, or finding common ground. It's about showing genuine interest and empathy.

3. **Reflect on the Experience**: At the end of the week, have your teen reflect on each interaction and consider these questions:

   ○ What did they learn about the person that they didn't know before?

   ○ How did showing empathy and understanding affect their connection?

   ○ Did they feel closer or more open toward that person?

4. **Prayer for Unity**: Close the activity by praying together for God to continue to help them build bridges with others, reflecting His love and unity.

Debrief: Remind your teen that building bridges means actively choosing understanding over assumptions and unity over division, mirroring how Jesus connected with those who were different.

Conversation Starter:

"Finding Common Ground and Showing God's Love"

Share a story with your teen about a time when you reached out to someone who was different from you or someone you didn't know well. Discuss how that experience impacted both of you, and explore together what it means to show God's love by building bridges. Use these questions to guide a conversation on the importance of bridge-building:

- "Can you think of a time when someone took the time to really understand you? How did that make you feel?"

- "What do you think are some of the biggest 'walls' people put up in relationships? How can empathy help to break down those walls?"

- "Why do you think God wants us to find unity with others, even those who are different from us? How does this reflect His love?"

These questions will encourage your teen to think about empathy as a tool for unity and for reflecting God's love to others.

WEEK 47

DEALING WITH GOSSIP AND BULLYING

Introduction:

This week, the focus is on addressing the harmful impacts of gossip and bullying and the importance of being a source of encouragement and protection. As you walk alongside your teen in this journey, guide them to understand the power of their words, the strength found in God's love, and the courage to stand up for what is right. Encourage them to be a light to others by fostering kindness, support, and bravery in difficult situations.

Practical Challenge:

Teen Challenge: If you notice gossip or bullying happening around you this week, choose to walk away from the gossip or speak up to defend the person being hurt. Be a voice for encouragement and protection, and let God's love shine through your words and actions.

Mentor Challenge: Be mindful of conversations around you this week. If you hear gossip, make an intentional choice to redirect the conversation or step away. Look for ways to show kindness and support to those who may be feeling isolated or misunderstood, modeling a spirit of encouragement.

Bible Story: Joseph and His Brothers (Genesis 37:12-30)

Reflection: The story of Joseph and his brothers provides a striking example of bullying within a family and one brother's quiet attempt to protect him. Joseph's brothers, fueled by jealousy, conspired to harm him, throwing him into a pit and selling him into slavery. This betrayal was an act of extreme bullying, born out of envy and bitterness. However, Reuben, the eldest brother, sought to intervene. Though he couldn't stop their plan entirely, his efforts to rescue Joseph remind us of the courage it takes to stand against mistreatment, even within our own circles.

Key Themes:

- Courage in the Face of Bullying: Reuben's decision to protect Joseph, even subtly, shows the importance of speaking up or acting against cruelty, even when it's unpopular or risky.

- The Consequences of Envy and Gossip: The brothers' harmful actions stemmed from their jealousy and conversations that fed negativity, illustrating how gossip and envy can escalate into serious harm.

- Hope Amid Adversity: Despite being mistreated, Joseph's story ultimately points to God's faithfulness, reminding us that even in the face of bullying, God can bring restoration and purpose.

Teen Devotional Recap:

- **Day 1:** *The Damaging Effects of Gossip on Relationships* – Proverbs 16:28 – Gossip can harm trust, cause misunderstandings, and break friendships. We are called to speak words that build up, not tear down.

- **Day 2:** *How to Avoid Participating in Gossip* – Ephesians 4:29 – Avoiding gossip requires intentional kindness and self-control. We are called to speak words that encourage and uplift others.

- **Day 3:** *What to Do if You're the Victim of Bullying* – Psalm 34:17 – If bullied, remember that God hears you and values you. Seeking support from trusted people can provide strength and perspective.

- **Day 4:** *Standing Up for Others Who Are Being Bullied* – Proverbs 31:8-9 – God calls us to be advocates for those who are mistreated, speaking up and offering support when we see someone in need.

- **Day 5:** *Seeking Help When Bullying Becomes Dangerous* – Psalm 82:3-4 – In serious situations, it's essential to seek help from trusted adults to protect yourself and others.

Weekly Summary:

This week, we discussed the harm caused by gossip and bullying and how we can respond as followers of Jesus. We learned the importance of using our words to build others up, standing against bullying, and seeking help when needed. God calls us to be a voice of encouragement and support, shining His love in every situation.

Journaling Questions for Mentor:

1. Reflect on a time when gossip affected a relationship or situation in your life. How did it impact trust, and what steps did you take (or could you have taken) to address it?

2. How do you respond when you witness gossip or bullying? Are there ways you can be more intentional about offering encouragement and support?

3. Consider a time when you were in a situation where someone needed defending. How did you respond, and how might you have acted differently?

4. What role does prayer play in dealing with difficult situations like gossip and bullying? How can praying for those involved, including yourself, help you respond with wisdom?

5. Are there specific individuals in your life you can be praying for who may be struggling with gossip or bullying?

Real-Life Story:

Nick Vujicic: Overcoming Bullying with Courage

Nick Vujicic, born without arms and legs due to a rare condition called tetra-amelia syndrome, faced significant challenges from a young age, including bullying. Growing up in Australia, he often felt isolated and different from his peers, which made him a target for taunts and ridicule at school. The hurtful comments and bullying made him feel like he didn't belong and led him to experience deep feelings of loneliness and despair. Despite the hardships he faced, Nick's faith played a crucial role in helping him navigate these difficult times. His parents instilled in him a strong Christian foundation, teaching him the value of inner strength and the importance of trusting God's plan for his life. In moments of bullying, he would often turn to prayer, seeking comfort and strength from his relationship with God.

One pivotal moment came during his teenage years when the bullying reached a peak. Nick was invited to speak at his school about his life and experiences. Although he was initially apprehensive about sharing his story, he decided to embrace the opportunity, believing it could help others understand his journey and perhaps foster empathy among his peers. As he stood before his classmates, Nick spoke openly about his struggles, his faith, and the importance of kindness. He shared how he found hope and purpose in God despite the challenges he faced. His vulnerability resonated with many students, and rather than condemnation, he received support and understanding from those who had once bullied him.

This experience not only helped to change the narrative around his life at school but also ignited a passion within Nick to advocate for others facing similar challenges. He realized that his story could inspire many people around the world. From that point on, he began speaking publicly about his faith and experiences, using his platform to encourage others to rise above adversity. Nick Vujicic's journey is a testament to the strength that can come from faith, resilience, and the power of vulnerability. Instead of allowing bullying to define him, he turned his pain into purpose, helping countless others find hope and strength in their own struggles. He says, "If you can't get a miracle, become one" (Vujicic, 2010). His message of love, acceptance, and faith continues to inspire people of all ages, proving that even in the face of hardship, we can rise and make a difference in the lives of others.

Discussion or Activity with Teen:

Activity:

Words that Heal

Take a moment with your teen to write down some encouraging words or affirmations that can counteract negative words. Talk about how words have power to either lift someone up or tear them down. Challenge each other to speak these positive words to someone who might be struggling or feeling isolated this week.

or

"Words of Encouragement Challenge"

1. **Identify Key Situations:** Encourage your teen to think of times when they've observed or experienced gossip or bullying, either in person or online. Ask them to consider how they felt in those moments and what responses might have been helpful.

2. **Commit to Kind Words**: Challenge your teen to identify at least three people this week to intentionally encourage — especially those who may be overlooked, teased, or left out. This could be through a kind note, a compliment, or a word of encouragement.

3. **Stand Up for Others**: If they witness gossip or bullying this week, encourage them to either change the conversation or stand up for the person respectfully. If it feels safe, they could try to shift the focus to something positive or express that they don't want to participate in gossip.

4. **Reflection and Prayer**: Afterward, reflect together on how they felt while encouraging others and how they handled any situations with gossip or bullying. Pray for God's help to keep being a light and to find courage in situations that need His love.

Debrief: Remind your teen that even small words can make a big difference, and standing up for what's right reflects Jesus' love and kindness.

Conversation Starter:

"Choosing Words Wisely and Standing Up for Others"

Share a story about a time when you were either hurt by someone's words or uplifted by an unexpected kindness. Discuss how those moments made you feel and explore ways you can help others feel supported, even in small ways. Guide your teen through a conversation about handling gossip and bullying:

- "What are some examples of how gossip or bullying can harm someone emotionally or spiritually?"

- "Why do you think God cares so much about how we use our words? How can we show someone kindness even when others aren't?"

- "How do you feel about standing up for others in difficult situations? What would help you feel stronger or more confident in doing so?"

These questions encourage your teen to consider the power of their words and actions and how they can courageously choose encouragement over gossip or hurtful words.

WEEK 48

HONESTY IN RELATIONSHIPS

Introduction:

This week, we focus on honesty, a fundamental part of trust in relationships. As you walk alongside your teen, help them understand the importance of honesty in building and maintaining trust, as well as the process of rebuilding trust if it has been broken. Encourage them to embrace honesty as a reflection of their faith, fostering relationships based on integrity and truth.

Practical Challenge:

Teen Challenge: Identify one area of your life where you need to be more honest, whether it's with a friend, family member, or even yourself. Take steps this week to speak the truth in love, ask for forgiveness if needed, and commit to living with integrity in that area.

Mentor Challenge: Identify a relationship where honesty can bring deeper connection or healing. This week, practice speaking the truth in love in that relationship. Whether it's sharing a difficult truth or simply being transparent about your feelings, trust God to guide you in each conversation. If appropriate, share this experience with your teen.

Bible Story: Zacchaeus and His Transformation (Luke 19:1-10)

Reflection: The story of Zacchaeus, a tax collector, showcases the power of honesty and transformation. Zacchaeus had a reputation for dishonesty, as tax collectors in his time often collected more than was required for personal gain. Yet, when he encountered

Jesus, Zacchaeus' life changed. He acknowledged his wrongs, repented, and committed to making restitution, demonstrating honesty and integrity.

Key Themes:

- Transformation Through Honesty: Zacchaeus' willingness to confess and make amends shows the power of honesty to change a life.

- Restoration of Trust: By promising to repay anyone he had wronged, Zacchaeus began the process of rebuilding trust with his community.

- Choosing Integrity: Zacchaeus' story reminds us that a life of integrity is within reach, even for those who may have struggled with dishonesty.

Teen Devotional Recap:

- **Day 1:** *The Foundation of Trust in Any Relationship* – Proverbs 12:22 – Honesty builds trust, which is the foundation of any healthy relationship. Trustworthiness pleases God and strengthens connections.

- **Day 2:** *How to Be Honest Without Being Hurtful* – Ephesians 4:15 – Speaking the truth in love involves being kind and considerate, sharing honesty in ways that uplift rather than harm.

- **Day 3:** *The Consequences of Lying or Deceit* – Proverbs 19:9 – Dishonesty damages relationships and leads to mistrust. Even small lies can lead to larger consequences.

- **Day 4:** *How to Rebuild Trust After It's Broken* – James 5:16 – When trust is broken, rebuilding requires humility, confession, and consistency. Forgiveness and patience are key to restoring relationships.

- **Day 5:** *Valuing Honesty in Your Friendships and Family* – Colossians 3:9-10 – Honesty should be a core value that reflects God's character, fostering genuine and trustworthy relationships.

Weekly Summary:

This weeks focus on honesty highlighted its importance in building trust, speaking the truth with love, understanding the consequences of dishonesty, and valuing integrity in relationships. Honesty reflects God's character and lays a foundation for meaningful connections built on trust.

Journaling Questions for Mentor:

1. How has honesty helped build or rebuild trust in your relationships?

2. When faced with a situation where the truth may be difficult to share, how do you balance honesty with love and compassion?

3. Reflect on a time when honesty strengthened a relationship in your life. What steps did you take to communicate truthfully?

4. Are there areas in your relationships where you might need to seek forgiveness or rebuild trust? What steps can you take to show integrity and consistency?

5. How can you encourage a culture of honesty in your family, workplace, or community?

Real-Life Story:

Abraham Lincoln: Honesty and Integrity

Abraham Lincoln's dedication to honesty is famously illustrated by an incident early in his career. In a case involving a man who was overcharged by a storekeeper, Lincoln discovered that his client had already been paid a significant amount, which meant he was attempting to extort more money. Despite the potential to earn a larger fee, Lincoln chose to tell the truth and advised his client to settle fairly. His honesty earned him the nickname "Honest Abe" and cemented his reputation as a lawyer of integrity. He believed that character and integrity were paramount. Lincoln's adherence to honesty, even when it did not benefit him directly, laid the groundwork for his legacy as one of America's most respected leaders. His example of integrity in the face of adversity continues to inspire many to value honesty and ethical behavior in all aspects of life, demonstrating that true character is often revealed in the choices we make when faced with difficult situations (Carwardine, 2007).

Discussion or Activity with Teen:

Activity:

Honest Reflection

Spend some time in quiet reflection and prayer with your teen. Individually ask God whether you have any area of your lives where you have not been practicing honesty. This could be something like not telling your friend that the show you've been watching together makes you uncomfortable, or surfing social media while you're on the clock at work, or not letting your sibling know that you used their stuff without asking them. If God brings anything to your minds, repent and ask God what you need to do to make it right. This may involve confessing something to someone and asking forgiveness, or having an honest conversation, or even confronting a situation that you've been ignoring. If it's appropriate, share with each other what God showed you about where you haven't been honest and what He is wanting you to do to fix it. Pray for each other, and then support each other in carrying out whatever God has asked you to do.

or

"Truth and Trust Building"

1. **Create a Trust Checklist**: Have your teen make a list of qualities that they believe build trust in a friendship or family relationship, like honesty, reliability, and respect. Discuss how each quality contributes to a strong, trusting relationship.

2. **Practice Speaking Truth in Love**: Choose a few scenarios together (like a friend asking for an opinion, a difficult situation at school, or an issue in their family). Then, take turns role-playing how to speak the truth with kindness and respect. Talk through how to balance honesty with compassion and how to address tough topics with love.

3. **Journal Reflection**: Ask your teen to reflect on a time when they were honest, even though it was difficult, and how it impacted their relationship. Encourage them to write about what they learned from that experience and how it influenced their view on honesty.

4. **Pray for Integrity**: End the activity by praying together, asking God for the courage to always be truthful and for wisdom to handle situations that require honesty with grace.

Debrief: Reinforce that honesty, even when challenging, is worth the effort because it builds deeper, more trusting connections and reflects God's character.

Conversation Starter:

"The Value of Honesty in Relationships"

Share a story from your own life where honesty either strengthened a relationship or helped you grow in a difficult situation. Discuss the lessons learned and how honesty, even when challenging, can build deeper, more meaningful connections. Encourage your teen to reflect on honesty's role in their relationships:

- "How have you seen honesty strengthen or, on the flip side, dishonesty harm relationships?"

- "What does it mean to you to speak the truth in love? How can we do this in a way that still shows kindness and respect?"

- "Are there areas where it's difficult for you to be honest, and how do you think practicing honesty could affect your relationships over time?"

These questions help your teen consider the importance of integrity and guide them in developing the courage to be honest in all areas of their life.

WEEK 49

HOW TO ENCOURAGE OTHERS

Introduction:

This week's theme focuses on the transformative power of encouragement and its role in reflecting God's love. In a world that can often feel discouraging, your teen's choice to encourage others can make a lasting difference. Guide them in recognizing the value of uplifting words, intentional acts of kindness, and the impact encouragement can have in challenging times. Share personal stories of encouragement and explore how God uses our words and actions to bring hope to others.

Practical Challenge:

Teen Challenge: Choose one person each day this week to encourage. Whether through words, actions, or prayers, find ways to uplift those around you. Let your encouragement reflect God's love and bring joy to others.

Mentor Challenge: Commit to encouraging three people this week through words, actions, or a simple note of appreciation. Think about how each person might need encouragement, and let them know how much you value them. Notice the impact it has on them, and reflect on how it strengthens your connection. Exchange stories with your teen and praise God for using each of you to bring joy to others.

Bible Story: Barnabas – The Son of Encouragement (Acts 4:36, Acts 9:26-27, Acts 11:23-24)

Reflection: Barnabas, whose name means "son of encouragement," played a vital role in the early church. Known for his kindness, generosity, and encouragement, he was instrumental in supporting new believers, advocating for Paul, and strengthening the faith of others. Barnabas saw potential in those others doubted and used his words and actions to lift others up. His life reminds us that encouragement can help people reach their God-given potential and grow stronger in their faith.

Key Themes:

- Advocating for Others: Barnabas believed in Paul's transformation when others were fearful, showing the power of encouragement to help people overcome their past.

- Supporting Faith: Barnabas strengthened the early church by encouraging believers, fostering growth, and building community.

- Recognizing Potential: Barnabas looked beyond others' shortcomings and believed in their future, encouraging them to step into God's purpose.

Teen Devotional Recap:

- **Day 1:** *The Power of Words to Lift People Up* – Proverbs 18:21 – Words have the power to bring life. Using words to encourage others can make a lasting impact on their lives.

- **Day 2:** *Recognizing When Someone Needs Encouragement* – 1 Thessalonians 5:14 – Observing others' emotions and behaviors can help you know when someone needs uplifting words or support.

- **Day 3:** *Small Ways to Encourage Others Daily* – Matthew 10:42 – Encouragement doesn't have to be big; small gestures can convey God's love and care to those around you.

- **Day 4:** *Encouragement as a Reflection of God's Love* – Romans 15:5 – God is our ultimate encourager. When we encourage others, we reflect His love and share His hope.

- **Day 5:** *Being a Source of Positivity in Tough Times* – Psalm 106:1-2 – Focusing on God's goodness helps bring hope to others, especially in hard situations.

Weekly Summary:

This week, we explored encouragement's power to bring hope and positivity to others. Through observing the needs of those around us, small acts of kindness, and choosing words that uplift, we can reflect God's love. Encouragement is a powerful ministry that strengthens relationships and points others toward God.

Journaling Questions for Mentor:

1. How has encouragement made a difference in your own life? Reflect on specific moments when others lifted you up with their words or actions.

2. Are there people in your life who may need extra encouragement right now? How can you show support in ways that reflect God's love?

3. What are some simple, intentional actions you can take to make encouragement a daily practice?

4. How can you model encouragement as a habit for your teen, helping them understand its value in friendships, family, and faith?

5. When has God encouraged you in difficult seasons? Reflect on ways you can share that hope with others in need.

Real-Life Story:

Henri Nouwen and the Power of Encouragement

Henri Nouwen, a renowned spiritual writer and priest, greatly influenced Nathan Ball, a young man grappling with his direction in life. Nouwen first met Ball when the latter was volunteering at L'Arche, the community where Nouwen served individuals with intellectual disabilities. From their initial meetings, Nouwen recognized in Ball a deep compassion for others and a strong sense of justice. During their conversations, Nouwen urged Ball to examine the dreams and desires he held close but had yet to fully articulate. With gentle but pointed questions, Nouwen encouraged Ball to consider what he felt called to do beyond societal expectations, emphasizing the importance of pursuing one's life calling, especially when it leads to serving others.

As Ball's mentor, Nouwen took a personal interest in his journey, often writing letters filled with encouragement and wisdom. In one of these letters, Nouwen told Ball to listen closely to his own heart and to be unafraid of taking the less conventional path if that was where he felt most alive and useful. Nouwen believed that God called people not just to succeed but to find meaning in service, and he saw in Ball a unique potential to do transformative work. This mentorship gave Ball a new perspective on his aspirations; Nouwen's guidance became a spiritual foundation that Ball returned to time and again as he weighed his options.

Ball ultimately decided to pursue his calling with renewed focus, eventually dedicating his life to working in community-centered missions. He credited Nouwen's mentorship as one of the pivotal influences that helped him define and commit to his path. Nouwen's encouragement to follow his dreams became a guiding principle, urging Ball to not only embrace his own gifts but also to support others in discovering theirs. This mentorship left a lasting legacy in Ball's life, illustrating how faith-driven encouragement can inspire someone to move boldly toward their life's purpose (O'Laughlin, 2009).

Discussion or Activity with Teen:

Activity:

Encouragement Jar

Together, create an "encouragement jar" at home. Write down positive affirmations, Bible verses, or words of encouragement on slips of paper. Each day, both you and your teen can pick a slip from the jar to read aloud, reminding each other of God's love and the power of uplifting words. You can then share those encouraging words with someone else during the day.

or

"Encouragement in Action"

1. **Identify People Who Need Encouragement**: Ask your teen to think of three people in their life who may need a bit of extra encouragement right now (a friend, a family member, a classmate, etc.).

2. **Create a Personalized Encouragement Plan**:

   ○ **Written Notes**: Have your teen write short, uplifting notes for each person they identified. The notes can include a Bible verse, a compliment, or an expression of gratitude.

   ○ **Acts of Kindness**: Brainstorm one small act of kindness for each person. This might be helping with something they need, spending quality time together, or sharing a kind word.

- ○ **Pray for Each Person**: Spend a few moments praying with your teen for the people on their list, asking God to help them find peace, strength, and joy.

3. **Deliver the Encouragement**: Encourage your teen to give the notes or perform the acts of kindness over the next week. Check in afterward to discuss how the experiences went and what impact they felt it had on their relationships.

4. **Reflect on the Experience**: Have your teen write in their journal about how they felt giving encouragement and any positive changes they observed. Encourage them to consider how making encouragement a habit can be a powerful way to live out their faith.

Debrief: Emphasize that encouragement doesn't need to be elaborate or formal; it's about being there for others in simple, genuine ways that show God's love.

Conversation Starter:

"The Impact of Encouragement"

Share a time when someone encouraged you during a difficult season. Discuss how their words impacted you and how God used that encouragement to bring you hope. Ask your teen if they can recall a time when someone's words or actions helped them feel supported and loved. Open up a conversation with these questions:

- "Who has encouraged you when you needed it most, and how did that affect you?"

- "What are some ways you can incorporate encouragement into your daily life, even in small ways?"

- "Why do you think encouragement is so powerful in showing others God's love?"

These questions can help your teen see encouragement as a meaningful way to support others and develop a lifestyle of uplifting those around them.

WEEK 50

BEING A GOOD BROTHER OR SISTER

Introduction:

This week's theme emphasizes the unique opportunity to foster loving, supportive relationships with siblings or, if there are no siblings, with brothers and sisters in Christ. Encourage your teen to understand that sibling relationships can be a significant source of joy, learning, and spiritual growth. As you discuss each day's devotional with your teen, share personal stories, memories, or lessons about sibling bonds, and explore how these relationships can reflect God's love.

Practical Challenge:

Teen Challenge: Choose one specific way to show love and support to your sibling(s) this week. Whether it's spending time together, helping them with a need, or praying for them, make an intentional effort to be a good brother or sister and reflect God's love in your family.

Mentor Challenge: This week, make an intentional effort to reach out to a sibling (or close friend) in need of encouragement or support. Spend time in prayer for them and find a way to show love through a specific action, like offering to help them with a task or simply spending time together.

Bible Story: Cain and Abel – The Dangers of Rivalry and the Call to Love (Genesis 4:1-10)

Reflection: The story of Cain and Abel shows the tragic results of jealousy, rivalry, and broken relationships. Cain's jealousy and anger toward his brother led to conflict, ultimately ending in tragedy. God calls us to value and protect our relationships with our siblings, learning from Cain and Abel's story to approach sibling relationships with grace, understanding, and love. This story encourages us to foster harmony and show kindness, knowing that these relationships are a gift from God.

Key Themes:

- The Importance of Unity: God desires harmony between siblings, not rivalry or resentment. Choosing love over jealousy strengthens the family bond.

- Being Accountable for Each Other: When God asks Cain about Abel, Cain responds, "Am I my brother's keeper?" God calls us to look after and care for our siblings as a reflection of His love.

- Handling Emotions with Grace: Cain's uncontrolled anger led to destructive choices. We are encouraged to handle emotions with maturity, choosing forgiveness and compassion over anger.

Teen Devotional Recap:

- **Day 1:** *What It Means to Be a Good Sibling* – Proverbs 17:17 – Siblings are meant to support and love each other through all of life's seasons.

- **Day 2:** *Showing Love and Support to Your Brothers and Sisters* – 1 John 3:18 – Love is demonstrated through actions, not just words.

- **Day 3:** *Handling Sibling Rivalry with Grace* – James 1:19-20 – Disagreements are natural, but they should be handled with patience, grace, and understanding.

- **Day 4:** *Encouraging Your Siblings in Their Faith* – Hebrews 3:13 – Supporting and praying for each other's spiritual growth strengthens the family bond.

- **Day 5:** *Being a Role Model for Siblings* – 1 Corinthians 11:1 – Your actions and character can inspire your siblings, pointing them toward a life that honors God.

Weekly Summary:

This week, we explored what it means to be a good brother or sister by focusing on love, support, and understanding. We learned how to handle conflicts with grace, encourage one another in faith, and set an example that reflects Christ's love. Sibling relationships are a special gift, providing an opportunity to grow, share, and love in a way that honors God.

Journaling Questions for Mentor:

1. How have your relationships with siblings or close friends impacted your spiritual life and personal growth?

2. Are there specific ways you've shown support, encouragement, or forgiveness to your siblings or friends recently?

3. What are some ways you can serve as a role model in faith, character, or compassion to those younger or newer in faith?

4. When conflict arises in your family relationships, how can you handle it in a way that brings peace and reflects God's love?

5. Reflect on a time when you encouraged a sibling or friend in their faith. How did it affect both of you?

Real-Life Story:

John and Charles Wesley: The Impact of a Brother's Encouragement

One powerful example of a Christian who had a significant impact on their sibling's life is Charles Wesley and his brother John Wesley. Together, they were instrumental in founding the Methodist movement, but Charles's influence on John's spiritual journey and calling was profound.

Charles and John were both raised in a devout Christian home, but each struggled with finding assurance in their faith. In 1735, they traveled to the American colonies as missionaries, seeking to deepen their own understanding of God and help others. Despite their good intentions, they encountered personal failures and discouragement, feeling that their work had not fulfilled the spiritual renewal they sought. The trip left both brothers searching for a deeper connection with God. Shortly after returning to England, Charles experienced a powerful spiritual awakening. While reading Martin

247

Luther's writings on the book of Galatians, he came to a profound understanding of grace and felt a newfound assurance of his faith in Christ. This experience transformed Charles, filling him with an unshakable confidence in God's love.

Charles shared this newfound faith with John, who was still struggling. With his brother's encouragement and testimony, John sought his own assurance of salvation. Just a few days later, John attended a meeting on Aldersgate Street in London, where he felt his "heart strangely warmed" and received the same sense of assurance in his faith. This experience became a pivotal moment in his life, leading him to pursue his calling with newfound zeal.

Together, the Wesley brothers went on to lead a revival in England that eventually spread worldwide. Charles's influence on John was vital in helping him find the spiritual assurance he needed to fulfill his calling, and their shared dedication to Christ changed countless lives. Charles, known as the "Sweet Singer of Methodism," wrote many hymns, while John became a passionate preacher and leader. Their legacy, built on the foundation of one brother's encouragement to another, continues to impact Christians to this day (Sprugeon, 2014).

Discussion or Activity with Teen:

Activity:

Siblings Appreciation Letters

Encourage your teen to write a note or letter of appreciation to each of their siblings (or a close friend if they do not have siblings). In the letter, they can express gratitude, share encouragement, and reflect on specific ways they appreciate their sibling's presence in their life. This gesture can foster closeness and deepen sibling bonds.

or

"Sibling Time Challenge"

1. **Plan a Shared Activity**: Encourage your teen to plan a small activity with their sibling(s), such as playing a board game or sport, watching a favorite movie, or helping with a task. The goal is to spend quality time together and enjoy each other's company in a way that builds their relationship. Encourage your teen to use some of the "deep" questions that they learned about earlier in the year (see Week 37).

2. **Pray for their Sibling(s)**: Set aside a few moments with your teen to pray specifically for their sibling(s). Guide them in praying for their siblings' needs,

struggles, and strengths, and asking God to deepen their bond and help them grow together in faith.

3. **Reflect Together**: At the end of the week, talk with your teen about how these actions felt and any positive changes they noticed in their relationship with their sibling(s). Discuss how they can continue to build each other up and support one another in small, intentional ways.

Conversation Starter:

"Strengthening Sibling Bonds"

Share a story about your own siblings or close friends who have influenced your life positively. Discuss the importance of forgiveness, patience, and encouragement in family relationships, and ask your teen to reflect on moments when their siblings or friends have supported them. Use these questions to help your teen reflect on sibling relationships:

- "What are some things you appreciate most about your sibling(s), and how do they make a difference in your life?"

- "How do you think God wants us to treat our siblings? What's one way you can show them love this week?"

- "In what ways do you think siblings can support each other's faith journey?"

These prompts encourage your teen to see the unique value of sibling relationships as a place to practice love, patience, and kindness.

WEEK 51

ROMANTIC RELATIONSHIPS

Introduction:

This week's devotionals guide your teen through foundational aspects of romantic relationships that honor God, focusing on love, boundaries, purity, and wisdom. Whether or not your teen is currently dating, these devotions can foster healthy perspectives and offer biblically based guidance for their future relationships. As you discuss each day's lesson, share your own experiences about keeping God at the center of romantic relationships, the value of setting boundaries, and trusting God's timing in love.

Practical Challenge:

Teen Challenge: If you are in a romantic relationship, take time to pray together and discuss ways to keep God at the center. If you are not dating, use this time to pray for God's guidance in future relationships and to focus on growing in your faith and character.

Mentor Challenge: This week, pray over your own relationships, whether they're romantic or platonic. Reflect on ways you can prioritize God's presence and set an example of love, respect, and commitment. If you're married or in a relationship, spend time in prayer with your partner, inviting God to strengthen and bless your relationship.

Bible Story: Jacob and Rachel – Waiting with Patience and Purpose (Genesis 29:16-20)

Reflection: Jacob's love story with Rachel is one of patience, commitment, and trust in God's plan. Although Jacob had to wait and work for years to marry Rachel, he remained committed to her, choosing to trust God with the timing. Jacob's patience and dedication show us the importance of pursuing relationships with honor and trust, even when things take longer than we expect.

Key Themes:

- Commitment and Patience: Jacob's story reminds us that love involves commitment and sometimes requires waiting. God's timing in relationships is often different from our own, but it's always for the best.

- Trusting God's Plan: Jacob's dedication to Rachel shows the importance of seeking God's will and being faithful to His guidance, even when challenges arise.

- Honoring God in Relationships: Jacob's love for Rachel was genuine and rooted in respect, setting an example of commitment that aligns with God's design for relationships.

Teen Devotional Recap:

- **Day 1:** *God's Design for Love and Relationships* – 1 Corinthians 13:4-5 – Love is selfless, kind, and patient, prioritizing honor and respect in relationships.

- **Day 2:** *Keeping God at the Center of a Relationship* – Ecclesiastes 4:12 – God's presence strengthens relationships, helping couples grow together in faith.

- **Day 3:** *Respecting Boundaries in Romantic Relationships* – 1 Thessalonians 4:3-4 – Boundaries protect purity and help build trust, allowing relationships to honor God.

- **Day 4:** *The Importance of Purity and Self-Control* – 2 Timothy 2:22 – Purity is about pursuing righteousness and relying on God for strength.

- **Day 5:** *Navigating Dating with Wisdom and Faith* – 2 Corinthians 6:14 – Seek relationships that encourage spiritual growth and share a foundation in faith.

Weekly Summary:

This week's devotions explore the importance of God's design for love, keeping God at the center, setting and respecting boundaries, pursuing purity, and seeking God's guidance in dating. Romantic relationships rooted in faith bring honor to God and foster spiritual growth, leading to healthier, more meaningful connections.

Journaling Questions for Mentor:

1. Reflect on a past or current relationship: How did keeping God at the center impact that relationship positively?

2. What boundaries have you found helpful to maintain purity and respect in relationships?

3. When have you experienced God's timing in relationships, and how did it help shape your perspective on love?

4. How can you encourage a young person to trust God's guidance in their love life?

5. What qualities do you believe are essential for a healthy, God-honoring relationship?

Real-Life Story:

Jeremy and Melissa Camp: A Love That Honored God Through Suffering

Christian musician Jeremy Camp married his first wife, Melissa, knowing she had terminal cancer. They chose to honor God through their short marriage, trusting Him even in the midst of suffering. Though Melissa passed away just months after their wedding, her faith and their commitment to God left a powerful legacy. Jeremy wrote the song "I Still Believe" during this difficult season, expressing his continued trust in God. Their story is a reminder that God-centered relationships are built on faith, trust, and love that go beyond circumstances. Even in heartbreak, Jeremy and Melissa's love reflected God's grace and purpose (Camp, 2020).

Discussion or Activity with Teen:

Activity:

Relationship Goals Worksheet

Encourage your teen to write down the qualities they believe are important in a future partner and the kind of relationship they hope to have. Include qualities such as kindness, honesty, respect, and a shared faith. Reflect on how these values align with God's design for love and relationships. Then, discuss how they can begin embodying these qualities themselves as they grow. Write down some specific steps they can take to mature into the type of person that is ready for a healthy, godly relationship when the time comes. Support them in setting realistic goals, and help them find additional resources on this topic if it is relevant to this time in their lives.

or

"Relationship Values Reflection"

1. **Define Relationship Values**: Ask your teen to write down a few values they believe are important in a relationship (such as honesty, respect, kindness, patience, etc.). If they're not currently in a relationship, they can reflect on qualities they hope to find in the future.

2. **Create a "Boundaries and Goals" List**: Encourage your teen to list some personal boundaries and goals that align with keeping God at the center of a relationship. They can consider boundaries that protect their emotional, physical, and spiritual well-being and help them honor God.

3. **Prayer for Future Relationships**: If they're comfortable, spend a few moments praying together. You can pray for wisdom, discernment, and a heart that seeks God's guidance in future relationships. If they're already in a relationship, pray for strength to keep God at the center and for God's direction.

4. **Reflect on Influential Relationships**: Suggest they think about a married couple they respect or look up to (such as family members or friends). What qualities in that relationship make it an example worth following? This reflection can help them think about characteristics that reflect God's love and values.

Conversation Starter:

"God's Plan for Relationships"

Share about your experiences with setting boundaries, waiting on God's timing, or growing in your faith within relationships. Discuss what it means to trust God in relationships, especially during difficult times, and encourage your teen to value patience, respect, and God's guidance. Use these questions to encourage a meaningful discussion on relationships:

- "What do you think a relationship that honors God looks like?"

- "Why do you think boundaries are important in a relationship? How can they help you stay focused on God?"

- "How can you see God's love reflected in a healthy relationship? What qualities make a relationship strong and faithful?"

These prompts encourage your teen to think deeply about qualities that make a relationship strong, healthy, and centered on faith.

NOTE: If you are your teen's parent and your marriage is not at the best point or you are divorced, this might be a sensitive topic for you. If you are going to have this conversation, be prepared to be honest about yourself, mistakes you have made, and things you would change about yourself. Do not speak about your spouse or ex-spouse in any way that would dishonor them.

WEEK 52

REFLECTING ON THE JOURNEY

Introduction:

As your teen completes this year-long journey, this week is about reflection, gratitude, and forward-looking commitment. Guide them in reviewing how they've grown spiritually, help them identify areas for continued development, and encourage them to set meaningful spiritual goals. Share your own reflections, goals, and areas of growth from the past year to model how faith is a lifelong journey.

Practical Challenge:

Teen Challenge: Spend some time in prayer this week, reflecting on the past year and setting goals for your spiritual journey moving forward. Ask God to continue to guide you, help you grow, and draw you closer to Him in the year to come. Pick a book from the **Resources for Further Study** at the end of this book to dive deeper into another faithful believer's story to help encourage you in your walk.

Mentor Challenge: Take time this week to write a letter to God, thanking Him for His guidance over the past year and expressing your hopes for the year to come. Use this time of reflection to set personal spiritual goals and pray for continued growth. Consider sharing parts of your letter with your teen to encourage them to do the same.

Bible Story: The Apostle Paul's Reflection on His Ministry – 2 Timothy 4:6-8

Reflection: Near the end of his life, the Apostle Paul reflected on his journey, saying, "I have fought the good fight, I have finished the race, I have kept the faith." Paul's life was filled with challenges, yet he remained faithful to God's calling. He looked back on his life with gratitude and hope, trusting that God's work through him would continue. Like Paul, as we reflect on our journey, we can be confident that God will carry on His work in us as we trust and seek Him.

Key Themes:

- Reflecting on Growth: Paul took time to remember the journey he'd traveled, recognizing both hardships and God's faithfulness.

- Gratitude for God's Faithfulness: Despite trials, Paul gave thanks for God's presence and guidance throughout his ministry.

- Continuing the Race: Paul's reflections remind us that while we look back with gratitude, we must also look forward with hope, trusting that God will complete His work in us.

Teen Devotional Recap:

- **Day 1:** *Reviewing Your Growth Over the Past Year* – Philippians 1:6 – Celebrate your spiritual growth and God's work in you, trusting He will continue to shape you.

- **Day 2:** *Thanking God for His Guidance and Help* – Psalm 100:4 – Reflect on God's faithfulness through both challenges and blessings, expressing gratitude for His presence.

- **Day 3:** *Identifying Areas of Continued Growth* – Romans 2:6-8 – Recognize areas where you still need spiritual growth, and seek God's help in continuing forward.

- **Day 4:** *Setting Goals for Your Spiritual Journey Moving Forward* – Proverbs 16:9 – Set goals for your spiritual journey and trust God to guide your path in the coming year.

- **Day 5:** *Committing to Keep Growing in Your Relationship with God* – Jeremiah 29:13 – Commit to seeking God with all your heart, knowing that a relationship with Him is a lifelong journey.

Weekly Summary:

This final week encourages your teen to reflect on the past year, thank God for His guidance, identify areas for growth, set spiritual goals, and commit to continuing their faith journey. Celebrating progress and expressing gratitude strengthens faith and prepares them to face the coming year with renewed purpose.

Journaling Questions for Mentor:

1. Reflect on your own spiritual journey this past year. How have you seen God at work in your life?

2. In what ways have challenges shaped your faith? How has God shown His faithfulness through these challenges?

3. What spiritual goals do you have for the upcoming year? How can you invite God into these goals and seek His guidance?

4. How can you encourage and support your teen as they continue their faith journey?

5. How can you make seeking God with all your heart a daily practice?

Real-Life Story:

Oswald Chambers: A Lifelong Pursuit of Spiritual Growth

Oswald Chambers, the Scottish minister and teacher best known for his devotional work *My Utmost for His Highest*, had a profound commitment to personal spiritual growth throughout his life. One notable story that exemplifies this pursuit occurred during his time as a student at the Royal School of Mines in London. Initially, Chambers had aspirations to become a painter and enrolled in the school to study art. However, during his time there, he experienced a transformative moment that shifted the trajectory of his life toward a deeper exploration of faith and spirituality. Influenced by a group of Christian friends and a growing interest in the teachings of Jesus, Chambers began to feel a strong call to ministry. This transition was not merely about a change in career; it represented a profound inner awakening. Oswald sought to understand God's will for his life, which prompted him to delve deeply into the Scriptures and engage in prayerful reflection. He would spend hours in contemplation, seeking to deepen his relationship with God and discern His purpose for him.

One of the pivotal moments in Chambers's pursuit of spiritual growth came when he attended a Bible conference led by the evangelist D. L. Moody. Moody's powerful preaching had a lasting impact on Chambers and confirmed his desire to serve God more fully. Inspired by this experience, Chambers made a conscious decision to dedicate his life to ministry, embracing the teachings of Christ with passion and fervor. To further his spiritual development, Chambers also immersed himself in the study of theology, church history, and the writings of other Christian thinkers. He was particularly influenced by the teachings of John Wesley, the founder of Methodism, who emphasized the importance of personal holiness and the pursuit of a deeper relationship with God. Chambers adopted these principles and integrated them into his own spiritual practices.

Despite his commitment to growth, Chambers faced challenges, including doubts and struggles with his own weaknesses. However, he remained steadfast in his pursuit, believing that personal growth was a lifelong journey marked by both triumphs and failures. He often wrote about the necessity of humility and dependence on God in his devotional works, encouraging others to embrace their own journeys of faith. Chambers eventually became a popular speaker and teacher, known for his deep insights and ability to articulate the complexities of faith. His writings continue to inspire countless individuals seeking to grow spiritually and develop a closer relationship with God. Through his own journey of personal spiritual growth, Oswald Chambers left a lasting legacy that challenges believers to pursue their faith with sincerity, dedication, and a willingness to learn from both their successes and failures.

Discussion or Activity with Teen:

Activity:

Year in Review and Goal-Setting Reflection

Choose an activity to celebrate the journey you have been on together, maybe a repeat of some activity you both really enjoyed during the year, or try something new — maybe GoKarts or taking an archery class. Together with your teen, review highlights from the past year. Use these prompts as a guide:

1. **Looking Back:** Reflect on a few key moments that shaped your faith this year. How did these moments help you grow closer to God?

2. **Challenges:** Identify specific challenges you faced and how you saw God's faithfulness in those times. Share moments you're especially grateful for.

3. **Future Goals:** Discuss your spiritual goals for the coming year. How can you each commit to keeping God at the center of your lives and seek His guidance?

Consider praying together to thank God for the past year and ask for His help in the year to come. Setting goals together can also strengthen your bond and provide mutual encouragement.

or

"Faith Reflection & Goal Setting"

1. **Reflection Journal**: Ask your teen to reflect on their spiritual journey over the past year. Have them write down moments when they saw God's hand in their life, how they've grown, and what they are thankful for. Encourage them to be specific, identifying any personal milestones, answered prayers, or spiritual breakthroughs.

2. **Spiritual Growth Assessment**: Have your teen consider the following areas of their spiritual life: prayer life, Bible reading, relationships, service to others, and faith in action. Ask them to rate themselves in each area (e.g., on a scale of 1-10) and identify what they would like to improve in the next year.

3. **Setting Spiritual Goals**: Based on their reflection, guide the teen to set 1-3 specific spiritual goals for the upcoming year. These goals should be both achievable and challenging, helping them grow closer to God. Encourage them to make these goals specific (e.g., "I will spend 10 minutes in prayer each morning," or "I will volunteer once a month").

4. **Prayer of Commitment**: Lead your teen in a prayer to dedicate their upcoming year to God. Ask for His guidance and strength as they pursue their goals and seek to grow in their faith. This prayer can be a personal moment or you can do it together.

Conversation Starter:

"Reflecting on the Year Ahead"

Express your gratitude for this journey and mention some highlights. Ask the following questions to prompt a reflective conversation about their spiritual journey and the coming year:

- "As you think back over this past year, what are you most grateful to God for?"

- "What area of your faith do you feel like you've grown in the most, and why?"

- "What's one area of your relationship with God that you would like to focus on growing in this year?"

- "How can I support you as you work towards your spiritual goals for the next year?"

These questions not only help your teen reflect on their progress but also encourage them to think about how they can take intentional steps to continue growing spiritually.

RESOURCES FOR FURTHER STUDY

Below is a list of books, websites, and resources where you can find more information about the individuals featured in the **Real-Life Story** sections of each week. These men and women have lived out their faith in powerful ways, and their stories provide great inspiration and encouragement as you grow in your own walk with God.

Week 1: Eric Liddell

- *Book: Pure Gold: Eric Liddell – An Olympic Champion's Legacy* by David McCasland

- *Website:* https://ericliddell.org/about-eric-liddell/

Week 2: Katie Davis Majors

- *Book: Kisses from Katie: A Story of Relentless Love and Redemption* by Katie J. Davis

- *Website:* https://katiedavismajors.com/

Week 3: Bilquis Sheikh

- *Book: I Dared to Call Him Father* by Bilquis Sheikh

- *Website:* https://peoplepill.com/i/bilquis-sheikh#google_vignette

Week 4: George Müller

- *Book: The Autobiography of George Müller* by George Müller

- *Website:* https://www.georgemuller.org/

Week 5: Brother Lawrence

- *Book: The Practice of the Presence of God* by Brother Lawrence

- *Website:* https://canonjjohn.com/2022/10/08/heroes-of-the-faith-brother-lawrence/

Week 6, 27: Elisabeth Elliot

- *Book: Passion and Purity: Learning to Bring Your Love Life Under Christ's Control* by Elisabeth Elliot

- *Website:* https://elisabethelliot.org/

Week 7, 36: Dietrich Bonhoeffer

- *Book: The Cost of Discipleship* by Dietrich Bonhoeffer

- *Website:* https://bonhoeffersociety.org/about/bonhoeffer/biography/

Week 8: Matt Redman

- Website: https://acsirevivals.wordpress.com/articles/heart-of-worship-matt-redman-story-behind-it/

- Website: https://www.youtube.com/watch?v=m83TSHhg-jU

Week 9: William Booth

- *Book: William and Catherine: The Life and Legacy of the Booths, Founders of the Salvation Army* by Trevor Yaxley

- *Website:* https://www.salvationarmy.org.uk/about-us/international-heritage-centre/virtual-heritage-centre/people/william-booth

Week 10: Joni Eareckson Tada

- *Book: Joni: An Unforgettable Story* by Joni Eareckson Tada

- *Website:* https://joniandfriends.org/

Week 11, 23: Hudson Taylor

- *Book: Hudson Taylor's Spiritual Secret* by Dr. & Mrs. Howard Taylor

- *Website:* https://omf.org/james-hudson-taylor-founder-of-cim-omf-international/

Week 12: David Wilkerson

- *Book: The Cross and the Switchblade* by Rev. David Wilkerson

- *Website:* https://tsc.nyc/david-wilkerson/

Week 13, 34: Billy Graham

- *Book: Just As I Am: The Autobiography of Billy Graham* by Billy Graham

- *Book: The Holy Spirit: Activating God's Power in Your Life* by Billy Graham

- *Website:* https://billygraham.org/

Week 14: C.S. Lewis

- *Book: Mere Christianity* by C.S. Lewis

- *Website:* https://www.cslewis.com/us/

Week 15: Smith Wigglesworth

- *Book: Smith Wigglesworth on the Holy Spirit* by Smith Wigglesworth

- *Website:* https://smithwigglesworth.com/life-in-the-spirit/

Week 16: John Newton

- *Book: Out of the Depths: The Autobiography of John Newton* by John Newton

- *Website:* https://christianhistoryinstitute.org/magazine/article/amazingly-graced-john-newton

Week 17: Brother Andrew

- *Book: God's Smuggler* by Andrew van der Bijl, Elizabeth Sherrill, and John Sherrill

- *Website:* https://www.opendoorsuk.org/about/our-history/brother-andrew/

Week 18, 47: Nick Vujicic

- *Book: Life Without Limits: Inspiration for a Ridiculously Good Life* by Nick Vujicic

- *Website:* https://nickvministries.org/

Week 19: Christine Cain

- *Book: Unashamed: Drop the Baggage, Pick up Your Freedom, Fulfill Your Destiny* by Christine Caine

- *Website:* https://christinecaine.com/

Week 20: Lecrae

- *Book: I Am Restored: How I Lost My Religion but Found My Faith* by Lecrae

- *Website:* https://www.lifeway.com/en/articles/ (Search "Lecrae")

Week 21: Max Lucado

- *Book: Anxious for Nothing: Finding Calm in a Chaotic World* by Max Lucado

- *Website:* https://maxlucado.com/

Week 22: Tim Tebow

- *Book: Shaken: Discovering Your True Identity in the Midst of Life's Storms* by Tim Tebow

- *Website:* https://timtebowfoundation.org/

Week 24, 39: Sadie Robertson Huff

- *Book: Live: remain alive, be alive at a specified time, have an exciting or fulfilling life* by Sadie Robertson and Beth Clark

- *Website:* https://liveoriginal.com/about/

Week 25: Lottie Moon

- *Book: The Life and Letters of Lottie Moon* by Lottie Moon

- *Website:* https://www.imb.org/about/lottie-moon/

Week 26: Bethany Hamilton

- *Book: Soul Surfer: A True Story of Faith, Family, and Fighting to Get Back on the Board* by Bethany Hamilton

- *Website:* https://bethanyhamilton.com/

Week 28: Samantha Ponder

- *Book: The Samantha Ponder Story: From Sideline Reporter to Football Countdown Host, Discover the Inspiring Journey of a Trailblazing Sportscaster Who Redefined Sports Media* by Regina Sharp

- *Website:* https://www.fca.org/fca-in-action/blog-detail/2017/11/06/6-questions-with-samantha-ponder

Week 29: Walt Disney

- *Book: The Man Behind the Magic: The Story of Walt Disney* by Catherine and Richard Greene

- *Website:* https://www.biography.com/movies-tv/walt-disney-failures

Week 30: William Carey

- *Book: The Legacy of William Carey: A Model for the Transformation of a Culture* by Vishal and Ruth Mangalwadi

- *Website:* https://www.imb.org/2018/07/31/missionaries-you-should-know-william-carey/

Week 31: David Green

- *Book: Giving It All Away...and Getting It All Back Again: The Way of Living Generously* by David Green

- *Website:* https://www.youtube.com/watch?v=2mjOHi-xDE8

Week 32, 42: Corrie ten Boom

- *Book: Tramp for the Lord* by Corrie ten Boom

- *Book: The Hiding Place* by Corrie ten Boom

- *Website:* https://www.corrietenboom.com/en/family-ten-boom

Week 33: J.C. Penney

- *Book: Fifty Years With the Golden Rule: A Spiritual Autobiography* by J.C. Penney

- *Website:* https://www.christianity.com/church/church-history/timeline/1901-2000/jc-penney-11630672.html

Week 35: Jim Elliot

- *Book: Shadow of the Almighty: The Life and Testament of Jim Elliot* by Elisabeth Elliot

- *Website:* https://www.christianity.com/church/church-history/timeline/1901-2000/jim-elliot-no-fool-11634862.html

Week 37: William Wilberforce and John Newton

- *Book: Amazing grace: William Wilberforce and the Heroic Campaign to End Slavery* by Eric Metaxas

- *Website:* https://washingtoninst.org/mentoring-a-georgian-era-daniel-john-newton-and-william-wilberforce/

Week 38: William Carey and Andrew Fuller

- *Book: William Carey: Obliged to Go* by Janet and Geoff Benge

- *Website:* https://banneroftruth.org/us/about/banner-authors/andrew-fuller/?

Week 40: Truett Cathy

- *Book: Wealth: Is It Worth It?* by Truett Cathy

- *Website:* https://time.com/3310038/rick-warren-chick-fil-a-founder-truett-cathy-truly-lived-his-faith/

Week 41: Tony Dungy

- *Book: Quiet Strength: The Principles, Practices, and Priorities of a Winning Life* by Tony Dungy with Nathan Whitaker

- *Website:* https://coachdungy.com/

Week 43: Mother Teresa

- *Book: Mother Teresa: Come Be My Light* by Mother Teresa

- *Website:* https://www.biography.com/religious-figures/mother-teresa

Week 44: Martin Luther King Jr.

- *Book: Strength to Love* by Martin Luther King Jr.

- *Website:* https://thekingcenter.org/about-tkc/martin-luther-king-jr/

Week 45: Fred Rogers

- *Book: The World According to Mister Rogers: Important Things to Remember* by Fred Rogers

- *Website:* https://www.dougdickerson.net/2019/06/30/leadership-lessons-from-fred-rogers/

Week 46: William and Catherine Booth

- *Book: The Life & Ministry of William Booth: Founder of The Salvation Army* by Roger J. Green

- *Website:* https://www.salvationarmy.org.uk/about-us/international-heritage-centre/virtual-heritage-centre/people/william-booth

Week 48: Abraham Lincoln

- *Book: Lincoln's Devotional: The Believer's Daily Treasure* by Abraham Lincoln

- *Website:* https://www.abrahamlincolnonline.org/lincoln/speeches/faithquotes.htm

Week 49: Henri Nouwen

- *Book: Henri Nouwen and Spiritual Direction: Wisdom for the Long Walk of Faith* by Henri Nouwen

- *Website:* https://www.americamagazine.org/faith/2016/10/05/spirituality-henri-nouwen-qa-gabrielle-earnshaw

Week 50: John and Charles Wesley

- *Book: John and Charles Wesley: Selections from Their Writings and Hymns* by Frank Whaling

- *Website:* https://www.christianitytoday.com/2008/08/john-wesley/

- *Website:* https://hymnary.org/person/Wesley_Charles

Week 51: Jeremy Camp & Melissa Camp

- *Book: I Still Believe* by Jeremy Camp

- *Website:* https://www.youtube.com/watch?v=5FMmxKM5Wj0

Week 52: Oswald Chambers

- *Book: My Utmost for His Highest* by Oswald Chambers

- *Website:* https://utmost.org/

These resources provide deeper insights into the lives of people who lived with boldness, faith, and love for God. Their stories can inspire you to live out your own faith with courage and commitment.

Feel free to explore these books and websites to learn more about the faith journeys, struggles, and victories of these incredible individuals. May their examples encourage you as you continue on your own walk with Christ.

SOURCES CITED

ACS International. (n.d.). *Heart of worship – Matt Redman's story behind it*. ACS International Revivals. Retrieved from

Sharp, R. (2024). *The Samantha Ponder story: From sideline reporter to football countdown host, discover the inspiring journey of a trailblazing sportscaster who redefined sports media.*

Billy Graham Evangelistic Association. (n.d.). *Billy Graham Quotes.*

Bonhoeffer, D. (2001). *Ethics* (K. W. Gros, Ed.). Fortress Press. (Original work published 1949)

Booth, W. (1890). *In darkest England and the way out.* Salvation Army.

Brooks, D. (2018, July 6). *Fred Rogers and the loveliness of the little good.* The New York Times. .

Brother Andrew, & Sherrill, J. (1967). *God's smuggler.* Chosen Books.

Caine, C. (2016). *Unashamed: Drop the baggage, pick up your freedom, fulfill your destiny.* Zondervan.

Camp, J. (2020). *I still believe: A memoir.* Thomas Nelson.

Cannon, M. L. (1997). *Lottie Moon: A biography of the revered missionary to China.* Broadman & Holman Publishers.

Carey, W. (1792). *An enquiry into the obligations of Christians, to use means for the conversion of the heathens.* Leicester.

Carwardine, R. (2007). *Lincoln: A life of purpose and power.* Vintage.

Cathy, T. (2007). *How did you do it, Truett?: A Recipe for Success.* Looking Glass Books, Inc.

Chambers, O. (2017). *My utmost for his highest*. Discovery House Publishers.

Curry, Izola Ware. The Martin Luther King, Jr. Research and Education Institute. (n.d.).

Davis Majors, K. (2012). *Kisses from Katie: A story of relentless love and redemption*. Howard Books.

Dungy, T. (2008). *Quiet strength: The principles, practices, and priorities of a winning life*. Tyndale Momentum.

Elliot, E. (1989). *The gate of splendor*. Revell.

Elliot, E. (1989). *Shadow of the Almighty: The life and testament of Jim Elliot*. HarperOne. (Original work published 1958)

Elliot, E. (2003). *Passion and purity: Learning to bring your love life under Christ's control*. Revell.

Graham, B. (1997). *Just as I am: The autobiography of Billy Graham*. HarperOne.

Graham, B. (2006). *The Journey: How to live by faith in an uncertain world*. Thomas Nelson.

Green, R.J. (2006). *The life & ministry of william booth: Founder of the salvation army*. Abingdon Press.

Greene, D. (2017). *Purpose over profit: How owning a business can change the world*. WaterBrook.

Greene, K., & Greene, H. (2016). *The man behind the magic: The story of Walt Disney*. Disney Editions.

Hamilton, B. (2004). *Soul surfer: A true story of faith, family, and fighting to get back on the board*. MTV Books.

Harris, L. (Correspondent). (2013). *The Chapel Hill News, Section: Chapel Hill News, Column: My View: Kindness makes a community*. Quote Page 1A. NewsBank Access World News.

Huff, S. R. (2020). *Live: Remain alive, be alive at a specified time, have an exciting or fulfilling life*. Thomas Nelson.

Jones, O. A. (1971). *J.C. Penney: The man with a thousand partners*. Ayer Company Publishers.

Jhe, G.B., Addison J., Lin J., Pluhar E. (2023). *Pornography use among adolescents and the role of primary care.* Fam Med Community Health. 2023 Jan;11(1):e001776. doi: 10.1136/fmch-2022-001776. PMID: 36650009; PMCID: PMC9853222.

King, M. L., Jr. (2012). *A Gift of love: Sermons from "strength to love" and other preachings.* Beacon Press.

Lawrence, B. (1982). *The practice of the presence of God.* Spire Books. (Original work published 1692)

Lecrae. (2020). *I am restored: How I lost my religion but found my faith.* Zondervan.

Lewis, C. S. (1955). *Surprised by joy: The shape of my early life.* Harcourt Brace.

Liddell, E. (2001). *Pure gold: Eric Liddell – An Olympic champion's legacy.* Discovery House.

Lucado, M. (2017). *Anxious for nothing: Finding calm in a chaotic world.* Thomas Nelson.

McCasland, D. (1998). *Oswald Chambers: Abandoned to God: The life story of the author of my utmost for is highest.* Our Daily Bread Publishing.

Metaxas, E. (2007). *Amazing grace: William Wilberforce and the heroic campaign to end slavery.* HarperOne.

Metaxas, E. (2010). *Bonhoeffer: Pastor, martyr, prophet, spy.* Thomas Nelson.

Müller, G. (1984). *The autobiography of George Müller.* Whitaker House.

Newton, J. (2003). *Out of the depths: The autobiography of John Newton.* Kregel Publications.

Nobel Prize Outreach AB 2024. (November 2024) *Mother Teresa – Acceptance Speech.* NobelPrize.org. .

O'Laughlin, M. (2009). *Henri Nouwen: His life and vision.* Orbis Books.

Piper, J. (2016). *Andrew Fuller: Holy faith, worthy gospel, world mission.* Crossway.

Pullinger, J. (2006). *Chasing the dragon: One woman's struggle against the darkness of Hong Kong's drug dens.* Hodder & Stoughton.

Redman, M. (2002). *The Unquenchable worshipper: Coming back to the heart of worship.* Regal Books.

Sheikh, B., & Schneider, R. (1978). *I dared to call Him Father: The miraculous story of a Muslim woman's encounter with God*. Chosen Books.

Sprugeon, C. H. (2014) *The two Wesleys: On John and Charles Wesley*. Wipf and Stock.

Tada, J. E. (1976). *Joni: An unforgettable story*. Zondervan.

Tada, J. E. (2010). *A place of healing: Wrestling with the mysteries of suffering, pain, and God's sovereignty*. David C. Cook.

Taylor, H., & Taylor, M. (1997). *Hudson Taylor's spiritual secret*. Moody Publishers. (Original work published 1911)

Tebow, T., & Whitaker, A. (2016). *Shaken: Discovering your true identity in the midst of life's storms*. WaterBrook.

Ten Boom, C. (1974). *Tramp for the Lord*. Chosen Books.

Ten Boom, C. (1982). *Clippings from my notebook*. Thomas Nelson Inc.

Ten Boom, C. (2006). *The hiding place*. Chosen Books.

Vujicic, N. (2010). *Life without limits: Inspiration for a ridiculously good life*. Doubleday.

Wigglesworth, S. (2002). *Smith Wigglesworth on the Holy Spirit*. Whitaker House.

Wilkerson, D. (1963). *The Cross and the switchblade*. Jove Books.

William Carey International Development. (n.d.). *William Carey Quotes*.

Acknowledgments:

This devotional was developed with the help of various tools and resources, including OpenAI's ChatGPT for assisting in organizing and generating ideas, reflections, and content.

www.ingramcontent.com/pod-product-compliance
Lightning Source LLC
Chambersburg PA
CBHW070912120626
46546CB00001B/235